CONCISE
LINCOLN
LIBRARY

—

EDITED BY RICHARD W. ETULAIN,
SARA VAUGHN GABBARD, AND
SYLVIA FRANK RODRIGUE

Praise for *Lincoln's Campaign Biographies*

"Thomas Horrocks has produced a comprehensive and thoughtful survey of the surprisingly voluminous but under-appreciated collection of campaign biographies about Abraham Lincoln that appeared in 1860 and 1864. Horrocks details how these earliest Lincoln narratives came about and then carefully analyzes their impact on his evolving national reputation. This is a must-have addition for the library of any serious Lincoln student."
—**Matthew Pinsker**, Pohanka Chair in American Civil War History, Dickinson College

"For the intensely private Abraham Lincoln, crafting an autobiography was nearly as painful as reading those campaign profiles written about him. As Thomas A. Horrocks demonstrates in this engaging and crisply written study, a series of political writers and editors faced uphill battle in selling the one-term congressman to a skeptical, divided nation, and then selling him again four years later to a war-weary public. Thoughtful, nuanced, yet succinct, *Lincoln's Campaign Biographies* can be read with profit by specialists as well as general readers."
—**Douglas R. Egerton**, author of *Year of Meteors: Stephen Douglas, Abraham Lincoln, and the Election That Brought on the Civil War*

"Thomas Horrocks shines a focused beam on the biographies written to promote Lincoln's presidential campaigns, turning them into wide-angle lenses that shed light not only on the critical elections of 1860 and 1864 but also on a wide variety of historical subjects, from the spread of print culture to the fall of the Whig Party. This is a revealing look at an important technique for making (or unmaking) presidential candidates in the nineteenth century."
—**Gerald J. Prokopowicz**, chair, History Department, East Carolina University

"Horrocks astutely recognizes that Lincoln understood the power of the written word as well as the power of photography; and that, as a politician, Lincoln expertly used the media and understood its importance to his political successes. Thus, the printed campaign biographies, with their deliberately evocative text and images of Lincoln, are valuable sources for historical analysis. As Horrocks correctly asserts, campaign biographies are 'a lens through which scholars can examine what party leaders, commercial firms, the American reading public, and, in some cases, candidates, thought were essential qualities of character and leadership' and how nineteenth-century Americans 'packaged and promoted these attributes.'"
—**Stacy Pratt McDermott**, *The Annals of Iowa*

"By putting Lincoln's adroit use of newspapers, photographs, engravings, and songs into the context of the rising interconnection among print, politics, and public opinion, Horrocks offers new insights into how the media of the time took the images of Honest Abe and the Rail Splitter and used them to introduce Lincoln to the Northern public."
—**Glenn W. Lafantasie**, *Journal of the Illinois State Historical Society*

"*Lincoln's Campaign Biographies* [is] an excellent book.... Horrocks describes presidential campaign publications such as almanacs, broadsides, newspapers published by political parties, illustrated magazines, sheet music, and songsters, which were collections of song in booklets ranging from 20 to 75 pages."
—**Henry S. Cohn**, *The Federal Lawyer*

"Horrocks expertly establishes the nexus of politics and a thriving print culture during the early decades of the nineteenth century."
—**Brian Matthew Jordan**, *Journal of the Abraham Lincoln Association*

"An impressive and seminal work of meticulous scholarship, *Lincoln's Campaign Biographies* is a welcome and invaluable addition to community and academic library Lincoln Studies and Nineteenth Century American Political History reference collections."
—*Midwest Book Review*

"Engagingly written and intelligently conceived, this brief study of Lincoln's campaign biographies throws new light on the campaigns of 1860 and 1864 and the creation of the Lincoln legend."
—**Martin P. Johnson**, *Journal of Illinois History*

THOMAS A. HORROCKS

Lincoln's Campaign Biographies

Southern Illinois University Press
Carbondale

Southern Illinois University Press
www.siupress.com

Copyright © 2014, 2024 by the Board of Trustees,
Southern Illinois University
All rights reserved
Printed in the United States of America

First printed 2014.
First paperback edition 2024.

27 26 25 24   4 3 2 1

The Concise Lincoln Library has been made possible in part through a generous donation by the Leland E. and LaRita R. Boren Trust.

Cover illustration adapted from a painting by Wendy Allen.

The Library of Congress has catalogued the 2012 hardcover and ebook editions as follows:
ISBN 978-0-8093-3331-8 (cloth)
ISBN 978-0-8093-3332-5 (ebook)

Library of Congress Cataloging-in-Publication Data
Names: Horrocks, Thomas A., author.
Title: Lincoln's campaign biographies / Thomas A. Horrocks.
Identifiers: LCCN 2024009240 | ISBN 9780809339600 (paperback) | ISBN 9780809333325 (ebook) | ISBN 9780809333318 (cloth)
Subjects: LCSH: Lincoln, Abraham, 1809-1865. | Campaign biography—United States—History—19th century. | Presidents—United States—Election—1860. | Presidents—United States—Election—1864.
Classification: LCC E457 .H828 2024 | DDC 973.7092 [B]—dc23/eng/20240227
LC record available at https://lccn.loc.gov/2024009240

Printed on recycled paper ♻

Southern Illinois University System

For Beth

CONTENTS

List of Illustrations xi

Introduction 1

1 Texts, Contexts, and Contests: Politics and Print in the Age of Lincoln 6

2 Constructing the Ideal Candidate: Campaign Biographies and Image Making 23

3 Promoting Honest Abe, the Rail Splitter: Lincoln's 1860 Campaign Biographies 45

4 The 1864 Campaign: The Rail Splitter as Father Abraham 77

Conclusion: Biographies and Ballots 101

Acknowledgments 109

Notes 111

Selected Bibliography 135

Index 143

ILLUSTRATIONS

Sheet music cover for Charles Grobe's *Lincoln Quick Step*   33

Cover of *Republican Songs for the People*, compiled by Thomas Drew   35

Cover of *Life, Speeches, and Public Services of Abram Lincoln*   49

Cover of the first edition of William Dean Howells's *Life of Abraham Lincoln*   53

Cover of Henry J. Raymond's *Life of Abraham Lincoln*   82

Cover of Orville J. Victor's *Private and Public Life of Abraham Lincoln*   84

Cover of William M. Thayer's *Character and Public Services of Abraham Lincoln*   86

Cover of anonymously written *Life of Abraham Lincoln*   87

Cover of *Abraham Africanus I*   95

LINCOLN'S CAMPAIGN BIOGRAPHIES

INTRODUCTION

On May 9, 1860, more than six hundred Illinois Republican delegates assembled under a tent, referred to as the "Wigwam," secured to the side of a building in the town of Decatur to nominate a gubernatorial candidate. Several delegates, including Richard J. Oglesby, arrived with an additional objective in mind: to secure unanimous support from the state delegation for the nomination for president of favorite son Abraham Lincoln at the Republican national convention the following week in Chicago. Oglesby, an up-and-coming Decatur Republican and future governor and United States senator, was convinced that Lincoln's rise from humble circumstances on the Western frontier would resonate with American voters, especially if tied to a popular image similar to those associated with Andrew Jackson ("Old Hickory"), William Henry Harrison ("Old Tippecanoe"), and Zachary Taylor ("Old Rough and Ready"). As far as Oglesby was concerned, Lincoln's nicknames "Old Abe" and "Honest Abe" by themselves fell short of what was needed to generate the levels of enthusiasm and excitement required to elect a relative unknown candidate president of the United States.[1]

Hoping to identify something in Lincoln's background that would lend itself to a captivating campaign image, Oglesby sought out Lincoln's second cousin John Hanks for a good story or two. All that the elderly Hanks could recall, however, was that some thirty years before, he and his cousin had split many rails several miles from Decatur. Hanks's recollection aroused Oglesby's curiosity, and days before the convention he asked Hanks to show him the split-rail fences he and Lincoln had made. Whether Oglesby sensed he was on to something before he saw the rails is unclear. What is known, however, is that when Hanks identified rails he and Lincoln had split and mauled, the two men tied a pair of them to Oglesby's buggy and took them back to Decatur, storing them in Oglesby's barn. A plan was then devised (with both men taking credit for the idea) to use the rails at the upcoming state convention.[2]

On the opening day of the convention, Oglesby and Hanks carried out their plan to link Lincoln with rail splitting. Before the voting for a gubernatorial candidate commenced, Oglesby introduced "an old Democrat of Macon County" to the assembled delegates. In walked Hanks and a friend carrying the two fence rails, decorated with red, white, and blue streamers and banners promoting "Abraham Lincoln, The Rail Candidate for President in 1860. Two rails from a lot of three thousand made in 1830 by Thos. Hanks and Abe Lincoln—whose father was the first pioneer of Macon County." The effect on the delegates, according to the *Illinois State Journal*, "was electrical."[3] As raucous cheering filled the Wigwam, Lincoln was called on to speak. After inspecting the rails, Lincoln, politely ignoring the inaccurate wording on the banners (the wrong first name of Hanks along with the false claim that Lincoln's father was the first pioneer of Macon County), confessed, perhaps a bit disingenuously, that he "did not understand this: I don't think I know any more about it than you do." Admitting that he could not be sure that the rails were ones he had split and mauled thirty years before, Lincoln claimed that "whether they were or not, he had mauled many and many better ones since he had grown to manhood." Lincoln's assertion concerning his rail-splitting prowess incited another outburst of wild cheering.[4]

Whether Lincoln had any foreknowledge of the staged event or even approved of it is unclear.[5] Yet whatever he thought of Oglesby and Hanks's dramatic maneuver, and despite his embarrassment concerning his humble origins and his dislike of farm work, Lincoln was an experienced and shrewd politician who understood the power of slogans and symbols, and undoubtedly he appreciated the advantages that the "Rail Splitter" image afforded his quest for the presidency.

Judging from the excitement generated at the state convention, so also did many of the delegates. Oglesby, Lincoln, and his supporters achieved their objective: passage of a resolution instructing the state's delegation to vote for Lincoln as a unit at the Republican National Convention the next week in Chicago.[6]

Of course, few delegates, party leaders, and seasoned political observers thought Lincoln had much of a chance of becoming the Republican nominee, despite his newly acquired sobriquet. Yet Lincoln and the team he assembled proved that nicknames and slogans alone do not make successful campaigns; a good candidate, competent managers, a compelling message, as well as one's own good luck and one's opponent's missteps are essential components. To the surprise of many, Lincoln and his Chicago convention managers brilliantly outmaneuvered the team working on behalf of the preconvention favorite, Senator William Henry Seward of New York, to win the Republican nomination for president. The Rail Splitter from Illinois, unknown to many in his own party, was now ready to be introduced to the American public.[7]

The nicknames "Honest Abe" and the "Rail Splitter" were now linked, and together they created a rough-hewn but potent image that was embraced enthusiastically by Republicans across the country. But the symbols of Lincoln's campaign possessed multiple meanings for many Americans, not just to those who identified with the Republican Party. The split-rail fence, particularly, was, in the words of one historian, "a powerful symbol in the nineteenth century," for it was "a distinctly American construction . . . almost ubiquitous in Lincoln's time." Moreover, the rail-splitter image resonated with a predominantly rural constituency in the North and West who identified with an ideology of free labor and adhered to a belief that one could improve one's station in life through hard work and self-discipline.[8] Prints, pamphlets, and newspaper stories linking the candidate with the axe, mallet, and split rails circulated widely in the weeks and months following Lincoln's nomination, evoking powerful images of hard work, the dignity and independence of free labor, and the West as a land where rugged individualism, economic opportunity, and the principles of democracy came together.

The image of "Honest Abe," while perhaps not as hearty and rugged as that of the "Rail Splitter," was just as wholesome, if not timely. In light of congressional investigations of corruption in the Buchanan administration, the theme of honesty hit home with many voters.[9]

The theatrical stunt conceived by Oglesby and Hanks in the days prior to the Illinois Republican convention gave rise to a dynamic image that helped enormously in electing Abraham Lincoln president in 1860. It gave birth to a movement that spread throughout the North and the West, energizing Republicans and attracting Free Soil Democrats and former Know Nothings looking for a new party, some even joining their former enemies as enthusiastic participants in Rail Splitter clubs and Wide-Awake parades and rallies.

It is not the purpose of *Lincoln's Campaign Biographies* to review Lincoln's election to the presidency in 1860 and his reelection four years later. These are subjects well covered by other works, including one of the contributions to the series of which this book is a part.[10] Rather, this work focuses on Lincoln's campaign biographies of 1860 and 1864 and explains the roles they played in shaping the Lincoln image. The genre of presidential campaign biographies emerged in 1824, when John Quincy Adams narrowly defeated Andrew Jackson in a controversial and bitterly contested election. Campaign biographies were one of several genres of print used to promote presidential candidates in nineteenth-century America.

In order to put presidential campaign biographies in perspective, chapter 1 presents a brief history of the critical relationship between politics and print in the age of Lincoln. An extensive and powerful publishing industry emerged in nineteenth-century America, aided by advances in communications, technology, and transportation; increasing literacy; the spread of mass education; and the rise of an urban, middle-class consumer. It is not surprising that the worlds of print and politics overlapped during this period. After all, political success in Lincoln's time depended upon not only running attractive candidates and drafting appealing platforms (relatively short documents compared to today's extensive party platforms) that addressed the issues of interest to voters, but on organizing and operating effective communication networks, in which print was an essential component. Thus print and politics were intertwined to the extent that the one sphere shaped the other. Politicians who failed to understand or ignored this relationship risked defeat and consignment to oblivion. More than most politicians of his day, Abraham Lincoln deeply appreciated and understood the influence and the power of print.

This close relationship between the worlds of politics and print influenced significantly the publishing industry, generating a variety of publications that were, to a large extent, ephemeral in nature, a mixture of genres directed to followers of one party or candidate and issued in conjunction with an election or a particular political event. Chapter 2 examines the rise of one genre of political print, the presidential campaign biography, as well as the common symbols and themes encountered in these works over the course of the century. Chapter 3 discusses Lincoln's 1860 campaign biographies and the image of a relatively unknown candidate they crafted, circulated, and promoted. The chapter explores how this image fit into the larger print campaign waged among the competing parties and compares Lincoln's image with those of his rivals as well as with the generic image of the ideal American leader formulated by writers of pre-1860 presidential campaign biographies.

Chapter 4 analyzes Lincoln's 1864 biographies. When he ran for reelection, the image and symbols that had attracted voters four years earlier remained relevant but were insufficient for promoting his candidacy to Americans enduring a bloody civil war. For one thing, as Lincoln completed a controversial first term in office, he was no longer an unknown figure. American voters had four years to form opinions and images of their president. Thus the purpose of Lincoln's 1864 biographies was to create a new image, a composite of a trusted father figure and the honest, rail-splitting Westerner created four years earlier.

The book's concluding section seeks to answer the question of what role, if any, these campaign biographies played in the election and reelection of Abraham Lincoln to the presidency.

CHAPTER ONE

TEXTS, CONTEXTS, AND CONTESTS: POLITICS AND PRINT IN THE AGE OF LINCOLN

On May 15, 1860, the day before the opening of the Republican national convention in Chicago, arriving delegates who happened to peruse that day's *Chicago Press and Tribune* were greeted by the paper's spirited endorsement of Abraham Lincoln for the Republican nomination for president of the United States. The endorsement, the editors asserted, was not motivated by a "great love and esteem for the man, by any open or secret hostility to any other of the eminent gentlemen named for that high office, nor by a feeling of State pride or Western sectionalism," rather by "a profound and well-matured conviction that his unexceptional record, his position between the extremes of opinion in the party, his spotless character as a citizen, and his acknowledged ability as a statesman will, in the approaching canvass, give him an advantage before the people which no other candidate can claim." The paper assured its readers that its support was not encouraged by Lincoln, for he was not, "by his own motion," a candidate for the office. "He has never sought, directly or indirectly, for the first or second place on the ticket." Rather, the paper was giving voice to a "spontaneous" movement of the people that "has sprung up suddenly and with great strength."[1]

Republican delegates as well as seasoned politicians who read the *Chicago Press and Tribune*'s advocacy of Lincoln would not, of course, have taken it on face value. After all, the paper was known for its strong ties to Lincoln and the Illinois Republican Party. John Locke Scripps, one of the paper's editors, was not only a friend and ardent supporter of Lincoln but would soon write a campaign biography promoting his candidacy. Moreover, few would have believed that Lincoln was, against his wishes, being pushed by the people to seek the presidency. In accordance with tradition, Lincoln had to show in public a disinterest in office. In private, however, he and his supporters were working hard for the nomination. His admission to Illinois senator Lyman Trumbull a few weeks earlier that "the taste *is* in my mouth a little" was an exercise in extreme understatement.[2]

A newspaper's blatant partisanship and a presidential candidate's public disclaimer of interest in the office were widely accepted—and expected—practices in Lincoln's time. In the nineteenth century, presidential candidates rarely campaigned personally. Actively seeking votes by giving campaign speeches, visiting towns and cities to participate in rallies and parades, and granting interviews to reporters did not become commonplace until the twentieth century. Thus, with candidates on the sidelines and out of view, it was up to the political parties to promote them and to craft and disseminate a message to energize and mobilize voters. By the 1860 election, political parties had become quite adept at these essential tasks, aided enormously by decades of party organization, a communications infrastructure supported by advances in technology and transportation, and the growth of a literate middle class.

The development of political parties as we know them today was not envisioned by the Founding Fathers when drafting the Constitution. In fact, parties, or *factions* as they were often called, were denounced by the nation's founders as antithetical to the tenants of classical republicanism, which espoused the virtue of the public good over the private interests of individuals or groups. Party alignments emerged during George Washington's presidency, however, as Alexander Hamilton, John Adams, Thomas Jefferson, and their followers split over differing interpretations of the Constitution, the role of the central government, and foreign affairs. But even as they formed opposing factions, Federalists and Jeffersonian Republicans (later becoming Democratic-Republicans) continued to condemn political parties as harmful to the nation. For example, Jefferson once wrote that if he "could not go to heaven but with a party," he would "not go there at all." The multi-tiered structures (national, state, and local) created to manage party affairs, articulate and communicate a national program, enforce loyalty, and identify and mobilize voters were not developed until decades later. The Federalist Party of Hamilton and Adams did not survive the War of 1812 and the Democratic-Republican Party of Jefferson was transformed into the Democratic Party of Andrew Jackson and Martin Van Buren.[3]

The Democratic Party that emerged during the 1820s, coalescing around the personality of Jackson, kept faith with a strict interpretation of the Constitution, limited federal government, state's rights, and a laissez-faire approach to economic affairs espoused by its Democratic-Republican predecessor. Under Jackson and his successors, the Democratic Party opposed internal improvements, a protective tariff, and a national bank while supporting Indian removal and an aggressive and expansionist foreign policy, the latter culminating in 1846, when President James K. Polk led the country into a war with Mexico. The vast territory gained by the United States as a result of that war ignited sectional conflict over the question of slavery's expansion. This divisive issue, submerged temporarily by the Compromise of 1850, rose again to prominence four years later when Democrats, led by Senator Stephen A. Douglas of Illinois, passed the Kansas-Nebraska Act, repealing the Missouri Compromise of 1820 that banned slavery above the Mason-Dixon Line while codifying the concept of popular sovereignty, which allowed residents of a territory—not the federal government—to make decisions regarding slavery. The political uproar caused by the Kansas-Nebraska Act weakened the Democratic Party as it split into Northern and Southern wings on the eve of the Civil War.[4]

The Democratic Party survived the Kansas-Nebraska firestorm, but the Whig Party did not. With several notable politicians among its ranks, including Henry Clay, Daniel Webster, and Abraham Lincoln, the Whig Party was formed in the early 1830s by opponents of President Jackson who believed he was concentrating too much power in the executive branch. Named in honor of English Whigs who opposed monarchical tyranny during the seventeenth and eighteenth centuries, the party advocated a strong legislative branch and a weak presidency. Unlike Democrats, Whigs were more nationalistic in outlook, favoring the federal government's role in the country's economic development. Many in the party promoted Henry Clay's American System, which called for the federal government to support a national bank, a protective tariff, internal improvements, and raising revenue through the sale of public lands. Whigs also tended to be moral reformers, embracing various antebellum movements, such as antislavery and temperance causes, inspired by evangelical Protestantism and a profound belief in the concept of individual and community self-improvement and responsibility. Unlike the Democrats, Whigs generally opposed territorial expansionism and many, including Lincoln, spoke out against the Mexican War. The Whigs quickly became a formidable force in American politics, winning two presidential elections in the 1840s. It was the passage of the Kansas-Nebraska Act in 1854, however, that administered the fatal blow to the Whigs, as many Northern and Western members left the party to join anti-Nebraska coalitions (from which emerged the Republican Party) opposed to the extension of slavery, while Southern members drifted into the ranks of the Democrats.[5]

It was during the 1830s and 1840s that both Democrats and Whigs developed party structures that twenty-first-century politicians would recognize. The Republican Party would do the same in the mid-1850s. County, district, state, and national committees managed party operations by identifying potential candidates, articulating campaign themes, drafting platforms, holding meetings and conventions, assembling lists of voters, identifying and providing speakers, raising funds, and mobilizing voters by organizing barbeques, parades, and rallies. Turning out voters and electing candidates required an effective and efficient communications network. Thus Democrats, Whigs, Republicans, and other parties established newspapers, cultivated editors, enlisted journalists, and published and distributed pamphlets, tracts, and other forms of printed material. None of this would have been possible, however, without the transformative advances in the realm of communications. This revolution in communications, according to one historian, was the "driving force" in the decades following the War of 1812 and continuing through the age of Lincoln.[6]

An effective communications operation was essential to the success of political parties in nineteenth-century America, when the worlds of politics and print were intertwined, each sphere shaping the other. Print's integral role in American political affairs dated back to the Revolutionary War, when almanacs, broadsides, newspapers, and pamphlets were used to promote the American cause.[7] But small printing establishments of the colonial and early republic periods, usually one-person or family enterprises, coping with tight credit, inadequate modes of transportation, and the difficulty of obtaining basic manufacturing materials, such as paper, could barely meet the needs of thirteen colonies let alone a rapidly expanding nation. For example, colonial printers rarely produced full-length books, be they original American works or reprints of English or European publications, because they were expensive to print and their price was beyond the financial reach of many Americans. As a result, a majority of early American printers, concentrated in the few large cities and towns, made a living not by producing and selling large, expensive books, but by selling stationery and proprietary medicines, serving as bookbinders and as postmasters, and by printing small, cheap publications, such as blank forms, primers, spelling books, broadsides, and almanacs.[8] Some printers also issued single-sheet newspapers directed to a local readership, the contents of which were devoted primarily to foreign news, merchandise for sale, and information on the arrival and departure of ships in the nearby harbor.[9]

An American publishing industry emerged during the decades following the Revolutionary War. The postwar economic recovery offered new sources of capital for entrepreneurial-minded printers, and the rise of political factions in the 1790s provided incentives for them to publish newspapers, pamphlets, and other genres of print. Moreover, the country's political leaders, convinced that an informed citizenry was an essential component of a republican form of government, supported legislation that helped build a national communications system. Congress passed legislation that created the nation's first postal system in which newspapers and magazines circulated at cheap rates and newspaper subscribers paid modest delivery fees. As a result, newspapers could be exchanged for free and their editors permitted to reprint at will material from other papers.[10]

The rise of an American publishing industry could not have occurred, however, without a base of literate consumers. The last decades of the eighteenth century and early decades of the nineteenth marked the beginning of what some historians have described as a "reading revolution," which was influenced by several factors that also fueled the revolution in print, among them: technological innovations in the printing trades (stereotyping, steam-powered printing, and papermaking machines) and advances in transportation (turnpikes, canals, steamboats, and the railroad system), communications (telegraph), literacy, and education. Literacy rates for both white men and women rose steadily through the first half of the nineteenth century, aided by the expansion of public and private schools, especially in the North, and stimulated by an "ideology of literacy," a notion that the ability to read and write was essential to moral and social self-improvement and democratic citizenship. The 1850 census reported a literacy rate of 90 percent among white men and women.[11]

Along with the increase in the numbers of Americans who could read was a rising demand for reading material. Those printers who strove to meet this demand by assuming the financial risks involved became this country's first publishers. By the 1820s printers had lost their place at the top of the American book trade to entrepreneurs—many of whom were former printers who gave up printing entirely—who were involved in publishing and book selling. According to one historian, there were some four hundred publishing firms, three thousand booksellers, and more than four thousand printing houses operating in the United States by the middle of the nineteenth century.[12] Increased demand for reading material led to intense competition among publishers to be the first to issue the same title or several titles on the same subject, while they struggled to outmaneuver one another and flooded the market with books and other genres of print. In order to survive, these publishers were forced to devise some cooperative mechanisms within the trade, such as exchange systems and commission sales.[13]

The rough-and-tumble publishing world of antebellum America evolved in an economy that was being transformed from one based on household production to one adapted to the marketplace. This "market revolution," as several studies label this transformation, wrought profound economic, political, and social changes that created new opportunities for some Americans and dislocation and disaster for others. Publishers, for example, operated in an intensely competitive and increasingly unstable economic environment. There was a fine line between commercial success, on the one hand, and bankruptcy and insolvency, on the other; capital, innovation, and the willingness to take financial risks in order to meet the growing demands of an expanding population of urban, middle-class readers separated thriving publishing houses from struggling firms awash in a sea of debt.[14]

Amid the advances in communications, technology, and transportation and the expansion of the market referred to above, publishers seeking income to fund several publications at the same time or merely trying to stay solvent increased their output of steady sellers, such as almanacs, primers, and, especially, newspapers. As Americans' demand for information and reading material increased, newspapers proliferated at a dramatic rate, becoming by the early decades of the nineteenth century the country's leading secular publication. In 1810, 365 newspapers were issued in the United States. That number increased to 861 in 1828 and reached 1,403 by 1840, representing a growth rate that outpaced the population explosion of the same period. While most of these papers were single-sheet weeklies, the antebellum period witnessed the emergence of the urban penny press and dailies, which were sold by newsboys for one or two cents per issue—and thus affordable for middle and working class readers—or were delivered to homes via subscription.[15]

Starting in the 1820s, newspapers became the favorite print medium for political news. Thus publishers found politics to be profitable on many levels in the decades prior to the Civil War. Aligning one's newspaper with a political party and producing pamphlets and other genres of print on the party's behalf provided not only financial backing and remuneration for a publisher and editor, but it could and often did lead to a lucrative patronage appointment or even to a political career. As was pointed out above, American newspapers were involved in politics during the 1790s with the rise of political factions that coalesced around Federalists and Jeffersonian Republicans, especially in the wake of the Federalists' Sedition Act of 1798, the purpose of which was to silence criticism of the Adams administration. But political newspapers of this period were founded primarily by elite party leaders to support or criticize a party in power and thus were, in the words of one historian, "a blend of court and factional press." Yet the opposition press that emerged in the 1790s, mobilizing voters for Jefferson's election as president in 1800, served as a breeding ground for a cohort of young printer-editors, including Thomas Ritchie and Amos Kendall, who later played influential roles in American politics in the decades to come.[16]

As the American political system became less deferential to elites and voting requirements were relaxed to broaden the franchise, politicians and parties moved away from the traditional practice of securing favor with other politicians in power and turned to direct appeals to the public through speeches, rallies, parades, conventions, and print, especially newspapers. Public events remained—and continue to remain—important for energizing and mobilizing voters, but in the nineteenth century their impact was limited by the size of the audience, the range that a speaker's voice carried, and the ability of people to hear. Such events were enhanced when they were promoted and covered by a newspaper, which enabled a much wider audience of potential voters to participate after-the-fact through reading privately at home or publicly in a hotel, post office, or tavern. In addition to covering speeches, conventions, and the like, newspapers reported on the pros and cons of pending congressional legislation, supported or criticized party platforms, promoted or condemned candidates, and communicated party news of a general nature. Writing in the late 1840s, one observer captured newspapers' centrality to the American political process when he claimed they "are to political parties in this country what working tools are to the operative mechanic."[17]

As newspapers became essential to the communications network of political parties, their editors, no matter how humble their origins or defective their education, assumed political influence and power never imagined by their eighteenth-century counterparts. National political organizations in which the press was an integral component emerged during the presidential campaigns and administrations of Andrew Jackson. From the presidency of Jackson through that of James Buchanan, political parties not only subsidized networks of newspapers on a national scale but sponsored and supported a national newspaper, based in Washington, such as the Democrats' *United States Telegraph* and *Washington Globe* and the Whigs' *National Intelligencer*.[18]

Editors of national party organs and other partisan papers became party insiders and leaders, roles they maintained through the election of Lincoln in 1860 and for decades after the Civil War. Amos Kendall, editor of the pro-Jackson Kentucky paper, *Argus of Western America*, set an early example of an editor acquiring political clout within a party. When Jackson won the presidency, Kendall not only was appointed postmaster general, but he became the president's speech writer and one of his most trusted advisers. Another example is Henry Jarvis Raymond, editor of the *New York Times*, who was one of President Lincoln's most loyal supporters among newspapermen. Named chairman of the Republican National Committee in 1864, Raymond wrote the first history of the Lincoln administration as well as a campaign biography of the president. Horace Greeley, longtime editor of the *New York Daily Tribune*, was an influential force in politics and reform as well as a leading voice within the Whig and Republican parties. He ran for president in 1872.[19]

In a 2005 work, Mark Neely shows the extent to which newspapers and other genres of print permeated American political culture: of some four thousand papers and periodicals published in the United States in 1860, 80 percent were political in character.[20] Over the course of the nineteenth century, voter participation increased significantly, averaging 78 percent in presidential elections, reflecting Americans' growing interest in politics during this period. And as more Americans became engaged in the political process, they demanded more political information.[21] And party operatives, acutely aware of the link between effective communication and voter mobilization, were eager to meet this demand.

The famous 1840 "Log Cabin" presidential campaign is a prime example of a political party, in this case the Whigs, using print in innovative and remarkably effective ways in devising and communicating a message to energize voters. Linked to a popular slogan, "Tippecanoe and Tyler Too," the party promoted its candidate, General William Henry Harrison, a man born into a wealthy Virginia family, as a rustic, hard-cider-drinking man of the people who wore a coonskin hat and lived in a simple log cabin. His opponent, President Martin Van Buren, whose origins were more humble than those of Harrison, was portrayed by the Whigs as an elite fop who spent lavishly on fine china for the Executive Mansion; a president out of touch with the American people struggling to survive an economic depression. The Whigs used every genre of print available to mobilize voters, including almanacs, pamphlets, campaign biographies, and special campaign newspapers, the most influential of which was *The Log Cabin*, printed in Albany and New York City and edited by a young Horace Greeley. Issued weekly during the campaign, *The Log Cabin* reached at least eighty thousand potential voters.[22]

While newspapers were essential to the mass communication network of political parties, they were not the only genre of print available to and used by party organizations. Massive quantities of pamphlets were issued by parties and politicians during the nineteenth century. Political pamphleteering, as Bernard Bailyn and Joel Silbey have ably demonstrated, was part of an American tradition dating back to the colonial era. With the emergence of the Democratic Party of Jackson, the Whig Party, and various third parties in the second quarter of the nineteenth century, pamphlets assumed a communications role second only to newspapers. Rarely more than thirty pages in length and cheap to produce in large quantities, pamphlets were usually paid for and distributed by national, state, and local party organizations at rallies and other political events. Congressmen used their franking privileges to mail copies of their speeches free of charge to supporters and potential voters. Often newspapers would reprint articles and speeches as pamphlets to reach a wider audience. Like partisan newspapers, pamphlets were used to disseminate a core set of beliefs; to educate and mobilize voters around a particular issue, platform, or candidate; and to denounce and ridicule an opposing candidate or party. Many of these publications were the work of anonymous newspapermen, party operatives, or party committees, and generally assumed a tone that was highly combative and polarizing.[23]

Another genre of political print used in nineteenth-century America was the campaign newspaper. First appearing during the 1828 presidential election, campaign newspapers were usually published in weekly installments between the nominating conventions and elections and were devoted to informing readers of the soundness of a particular party's platform and the superior strengths of its candidate while heaping invective and ridicule on the opposing party and its standard bearer. Issued either as an offshoot of an established partisan newspaper or an independent venture initiated and funded by a party or a party supporter, campaign newspapers' sole purpose was to educate and energize voters. Two of the better known 1860 Lincoln campaign newspapers, each named *The Rail Splitter*, were published in Chicago and Cincinnati respectively and edited by local Republican supporters.[24]

As with campaign newspapers, presidential campaign biographies were published every four years, usually between the summer nominating conventions and the fall elections. Dating back to the 1824 election between John Quincy Adams and Andrew Jackson, candidate biographies, produced by political parties as well as by commercial firms, have appeared in every presidential campaign since that controversial contest. (Campaign biographies will be treated in greater depth in chapter 2.)

Campaign newspapers and candidate biographies were advertised in national as well as local newspapers, along with other forms of printed material, such as partisan almanacs; engravings and lithographs of presidential candidates; sheet music and songsters; cartoons; and, by the middle of the century, photographs. It is important to note, however, that political parties and partisans did not monopolize the production of these various forms of printed material. Taking advantage of advances in printing technology and transportation as well the rise of an urban, middle-class consumer, commercial firms and entrepreneurs were, by the 1840s, active in producing printed material of a political nature. Not so much competing against political organizations as aiding and abetting them, commercial publishing houses and printing firms pursued an agenda that was driven by profit rather than by politics. Whereas political organizations produced material in order to persuade and mobilize voters to cast ballots for a particular candidate or party, commercial firms tended to be nonpartisan, publishing books, engravings, or sheet music that promoted the fortunes of every candidate in the race. After all, it made good business sense to meet the needs of potential clients regardless of their political persuasion.

One such firm that possessed a firm grasp of the interests of American middle-class consumers was Currier and Ives. According to a historian of the firm, Currier and Ives did not lead public opinion, rather they reflected it. Best known today for their romanticized and sentimental depictions of nineteenth-century American small town life, Currier and Ives, sensitive to American's intense interest in politics, produced numerous political prints, many in color, from the 1840s through the 1890s, including election "banners," featuring presidential and vice-presidential candidates for each party; portraits of presidents, presidential candidates, and other political figures; and cartoons. Some, of course, may have been produced on commission, but many were issued in response to popular demand. The firm published more than 250 political prints over the span of its lifetime; its lithographic portraits of politicians were generally issued in small or medium folio size, implying that they were made to be framed and hung in the home.[25]

Framed prints, intended to be displayed in the parlor of a middle-class home, not only drew attention to one's attainment of social and economic respectability but also to one's political loyalties. The parlor, used for family gatherings and for entertaining guests, might also contain a piano and sheet music. The latter was another genre of nineteenth-century print issued by commercial firms that appealed to the American public's interest in politics and political figures. Music played an important role in American political campaigns from the beginning of the nineteenth century, and sheet music, particularly, was used to promote candidates and energize their supporters through participation in dancing and singing. During the 1840 presidential campaign, for example, a number of companies published sheet music in support of Whig nominee William Henry Harrison under such titles as the *Tippecanoe Waltz*, *The Log Cabin Quick Step*, and the *Tippecanoe Hornpipe*. Twenty years later, Abraham Lincoln's presidential quest was promoted by *Honest Old Abe*, *Lincoln's Grand March*, and the *Lincoln Polka*, to name but a few. Sheet music often included a wood engraving or lithographic print of a candidate on the cover, thus providing the American public with a rare opportunity, in an age before photography, to see what candidates looked like.[26]

Related to sheet music was the songster, another genre of print that became a staple of nineteenth-century American political campaigns. A collection of songs in a booklet ranging anywhere from twenty to seventy-five pages in length, songsters were inexpensive to produce and small enough to fit in one's pocket. Two examples are Weeks, Jordan and Company's *Harrison Melodies*, a seventy-two-page publication containing some fifty songs promoting the 1840 Whig presidential candidate, and *The Rough and Ready Songster*, espousing the election of the 1848 Whig candidate Zachary Taylor. Containing lyrics written specifically for a campaign and set to traditional or well-known melodies, such as *Yankee Doodle* and *Auld Lang Syne*, songsters were intended to be used in marches, parades, and rallies. Songsters, too, often included woodcut portraits of candidates on their covers.[27]

Illustrated newspapers, most notably *Frank Leslie's Illustrated Newspaper* and *Harper's Weekly*, were born in the 1850s, and their rise brought forth a steady stream of woodcuts and engravings of a political nature, including cartoons. Unlike the dignified engravings and lithographs of candidates and other political luminaries that were created to be hung in the home, cartoons used jest, ridicule, biting satire, and bawdy humor in their depictions of candidates. If political cartoons were meant to be hung, it was certainly not in the parlor where they would be seen by women and children, but rather on the walls of a party clubhouse or a public space frequented primarily by men.[28]

Harper's Weekly, Frank Leslie's Illustrated News, the *New York Illustrated News*, and other illustrated newspapers included cartoons among its numerous serious depictions of political figures and events. These illustrated publications were made possible by the development of photography. Though not yet able to reproduce photographs, newspapers and periodicals could, by the 1860 campaign, print lithographs and engravings of candidates, parades, conventions, and the like created by news artists from photographs. Advances in photography and printing impacted all genres of print. Moreover, by the 1860 election, the carte de visite photograph and albums to house them had become popular with Americans. Now individuals and families could assemble collections of photographic images not just of family and friends but also of their favorite statesmen and politicians.[29]

Few nineteenth-century American politicians understood the relationship between politics and print and the power of the printed word as well as Abraham Lincoln. Born into humble circumstances and receiving a formal education lasting less than a year, Lincoln was a life-long autodidact; he virtually read his way out of the primitive frontier environment of his youth through a vigorous self-improvement regimen. In an 1859 lecture on "Discoveries and Inventions," Lincoln acknowledged the critical importance of printing in history: "At length printing came. It gave ten thousand copies of any written matter, quite cheaply as ten were given before; and consequently a thousand minds were brought into the field where there was but one before. This was a great *gain*; and history shows a great *change* corresponding to it, in point of time. I will venture to consider *it*, the true termination of that period called 'the dark ages.'"[30]

Lincoln developed into a shrewd politician with an astute comprehension of the power of public opinion. Once claiming that "Public opinion in this country is everything," Lincoln told a group of Republicans that "Our government rests on public opinion. Whoever can change public opinion, can change the government, practically just so much."[31] Keenly appreciating the role of print in shaping public opinion, Lincoln, from the beginning of his political career in both New Salem and Springfield, Illinois, and through his years as president, used print, especially newspapers, to further his and his party's agenda. A contributor of hundreds of anonymous and pseudonymous editorials to Springfield's *Sangamo Journal* and *Illinois State Journal*, Lincoln courted newspaper editors when he ran for Congress in 1846 and used print in general and the Whig press in particular during his single term in the U.S. House of Representatives to publish and circulate his speeches. And like his fellow congressmen, he used to his advantage franking privileges to mail printed versions of his speeches to constituents back home in Illinois.[32]

In the 1840 presidential campaign, Lincoln worked hard in Illinois for Whig candidate William Henry Harrison, including serving as one of the editors of the *Old Soldier*, a Harrison campaign newspaper.[33] Twenty years later, Lincoln, acutely sensitive to the advantage of gaining support of a growing German Protestant community, secretly purchased a Springfield German-language newspaper, the *Illinois Staats-Anzeiger*. In addition to acquiring a printing press and German type, Lincoln brought in a German-American editor, Theodore Canisius, to run the pro-Republican paper. He understood that certain anti-immigrant Whig and Republican policies, especially in the Northeast, had alienated this swing-vote constituency. Moreover, William Seward, Lincoln's chief rival for the Republican nomination for president, had attracted favorable attention among German Americans as a result of his support of immigrants and his opposition to the Know-Nothing Party movement.[34]

In the wake of his 1858 senate campaign against Stephen Douglas and fully aware of the positive publicity he received as a result his debate performances, Lincoln labored diligently to get the debates published. He assembled a scrapbook containing newspaper accounts and transcripts of the debates and, with the assistance of the Ohio Republican Committee, found an Ohio firm, Follett and Foster, to publish the debates in book form. The debates were published on the eve of the 1860 Republican convention in Chicago in mid-May and became an instant best-seller, going through four printings within weeks of its first appearance.[35] Lincoln also made sure that print editions of his Cooper Union address in New York City earlier in the year would be not only widely disseminated but accurately recorded.

Appreciating the distinct advantages of having his speech published in various New York newspapers and subsequently in pamphlet form, Lincoln visited the *New York Daily Tribune* office after his speech to read galley proof and corrected galley proof before it appeared in press the next morning. The pamphlet version of the speech was issued in September, weeks before the election, and, like the published Lincoln-Douglas debates, aided Lincoln enormously, selling more than 850,000 copies.[36]

Lincoln's campaign for president was promoted by numerous newspaper editors, many of whom he cultivated assiduously during his career. He used his close relationship with the *Chicago Press and Tribune* to secure its public support of his nomination for president the day before the opening of the Republican convention in Chicago, and he provided one of the paper's editors, John Lock Scripps, with an autobiographical sketch to be issued as a campaign biography for the general election. Once in the White House, Lincoln did not forget his friends in the press and publishing field, dispensing patronage positions and diplomatic appointments to more editors, journalists, and publishers than any of his predecessors had ever done. As president, he broke with tradition by not establishing an official administration newspaper in the nation's capital, preferring to use various editors and newspapers to disseminate information and shape public opinion. Lincoln's use of public letters to communicate with the American people via the press proved brilliantly effective in building support on key issues, such as emancipation and the suspension of habeas corpus. When responding to Horace Greeley's August 20, 1862, editorial in the *New York Daily Tribune*, which scolded the president for his slowness on emancipation, Lincoln chose to respond to Greeley not in the editor's own paper but in the rival *National Intelligencer*, thus giving the editors of both papers notice that he would give or withhold news based on support of his administration.[37]

Lincoln possessed a thick skin for a politician, rarely taking political attacks personally. And there were plenty of vicious assaults, not only against his policies but aimed at him personally, that appeared in print, especially in newspapers. Lincoln could easily have used his war powers to quash opposition newspapers and to arrest disloyal publishers. He was, in general, firmly committed to the concept of an opposition press and thus opposed to widespread arrests of Democratic and Copperhead editors or the closing down of antiwar newspapers. To be sure, such arrests and actions did occur, but they proved to be the exception rather than the norm.[38]

Finally, it must be noted that Lincoln early on appreciated the power of photography. While in New York City to give his Cooper Union address, he stopped by the photography studio of Mathew Brady, who produced what became, in the words of one historian, "a campaign icon." Brady's photograph, presenting the rough-hewn Westerner as a dignified statesmen, was mass produced in numerous prints, books, cartoons, broadsides, and campaign pins.[39]

CHAPTER TWO

CONSTRUCTING THE IDEAL CANDIDATE: CAMPAIGN BIOGRAPHIES AND IMAGE MAKING

Jesse W. Fell, a lawyer and politician from Bloomington, Illinois, had by 1858 known Abraham Lincoln for more than twenty years. Like his friend Lincoln, Fell originally was a Whig in the Henry Clay mold before joining the Republican Party in the wake of the Kansas-Nebraska firestorm. Impressed with Lincoln's performance in the 1858 debates with Stephen Douglas, Fell was convinced, as were a growing number of Illinois Republicans, that the tall Springfield lawyer's future was on the national political stage. "Seriously, Lincoln," Fell informed his fellow Republican, "Your discussion with Judge Douglas has demonstrated your ability and your devotion to freedom; you have no embarrassing record; you have sprung from the humble walks of life, sharing in its toils and trials; and if only we can get these facts sufficiently before the people, depend on it, there is a chance for you." Fell, willing to assist in disseminating the Lincoln story, asked his friend for an autobiographical narrative. After initially turning down Fell's request, Lincoln eventually complied a year later, sending a brief sketch of 606 words, explaining that "There is not much of it, for the reason, I suppose, that there is not much of me."[1]

Lincoln made it clear to Fell that the sketch "must not appear to have been written by myself," an understandable request by a politician wanting to convey an appearance of disinterest in popularity and in seeking office. He also asked Fell that if anything "be made" of the autobiography, "I wish it to be modest, and not go beyond the materials. If it were thought necessary to incorporate any thing from any of my speeches, I suppose there would be no objection." This request was ignored, for if there was anything "to be made" of Lincoln's scanty, unadorned, and uninspired sketch, it would require some degree of embellishment on Fell's part. Fell, a native Pennsylvanian who understood the importance of that state in the upcoming presidential election, sent Lincoln's autobiographical piece on to his friend Joseph J. Lewis, a Republican activist in West Chester, Pennsylvania, so that the latter could circulate the Lincoln story among the party faithful. Lewis rewrote and enhanced Lincoln's sparse sketch in order to make it appealing, especially to his fellow Pennsylvanians. Nearly three thousand words in length, Lewis's biography of Lincoln was published in the *Chester County Times* on February 11, 1860, subsequently reprinted in other Republican newspapers, and served as the basis of the first biographical accounts of Lincoln after he won the Republican nomination for president in Chicago in May of that year.[2]

Lewis's account touted Lincoln as a superb debater and orator, a successful lawyer whose courtroom arguments "were masterpieces of logical reasoning," a strong advocate of a protective tariff, and as one of the "first to join in the formation of the Republican party." While Lincoln would not have disputed any of these statements, he did not include them in his sketch. In fact, he ended his autobiographical sketch in 1854, with the passage of the Kansas-Nebraska Act, passing over his recent political activities, including his famous debates with Douglas because they were "pretty well known." What is notable about both Lincoln's and Lewis's versions is the absence of key elements of the Lincoln image that would be crafted and promoted by the Republican Party and by commercial publishers in the 1860 presidential campaign. Lewis's biography first appeared several months before the Illinois Republican convention, which gave birth to the rail-splitter image that was merged with Lincoln's reputation for honesty.[3] After receiving the Republican nomination for president, Lincoln composed a longer autobiographical account that reflected not only his enhanced political stature but a political landscape that had changed dramatically since he sent Fell his brief autobiography more than a year before. As will be shown in the next chapter, Lincoln's second autobiographical account also would be embellished by others, but this time it would be molded into a carefully crafted image that conformed to a formula established by presidential campaign biographies published over the previous thirty-six years.

Emerging from the Republican convention as his party's nominee for president of the United States, Abraham Lincoln followed tradition, remaining in Springfield and refraining from public campaigning. Private campaigning, of course, was another matter; working out of the governor's office at the Illinois statehouse, Lincoln met regularly with close advisers, party operatives, Republican leaders, and friendly editors and journalists over the course of the campaign. Ever the sagacious politician, Lincoln was not about to let others run his campaign. Turning his law practice over to his assistant, William Henry Herndon, and hiring the young German-born journalist John Nicolay as his secretary, Lincoln worked actively behind the scenes on campaign strategy, keeping in constant communication with campaign managers and operatives, especially those working in swing states and with key swing-vote constituencies, such as German Americans, and following newspaper accounts and editorials. An inveterate reader of newspapers, Lincoln understood the power of print in the political realm. He used his relationships with many newspaper editors to place articles and editorials supportive of the Republican cause.[4]

By the end of June 1860, there were three candidates running for president in addition to Lincoln: Stephen A. Douglas of Illinois representing the Northern wing of the Democratic Party, John C. Breckinridge of Kentucky, the nominee of the Southern wing of the Democratic Party, and John Bell of Tennessee, the choice of the Constitutional Union Party. With the Democratic Party split into two regional factions, Lincoln and the Republican Party were optimistic about the election. They were not taking any chances, however. The party's platform, opposing the extension of slavery in the territories, endorsing a Hamiltonian-Whig economic program consisting of a protective tariff, internal improvements, and construction of a Pacific Railroad, as well as espousing the rights of immigrants and naturalized citizens, was linked to a moderate antislavery candidate with an appealing life story. The Republican press, complemented by nonpartisan entrepreneurs and publishers, made sure American voters became acquainted with the little known Westerner who was heading the party's ticket by vigorously promoting the Lincoln story and the images and symbols that brought that story vividly to life.[5]

The image of Lincoln that emerged from the Decatur and Chicago conventions was disseminated widely through books, pamphlets, newspapers, songs, and other genres of print. Richard Oglesby may have thought Lincoln's sobriquet "Honest Old Abe" was by itself inadequate to motivate Americans to vote for his friend, but many other party supporters and journalists thought otherwise, seeing Lincoln's reputation for honesty as an advantage in swing states, such as Pennsylvania, especially in light of alleged corruption associated with the Buchanan administration. One writer, in a brief article that appeared in a Chicago Republican campaign newspaper, the *Rail Splitter*, was direct and to the point, averring that Lincoln "never incurs debts when he has the means to pay. And at the present time he owes no man a dollar. There are few public men, we think, who can fill this bill of qualities." "Look upon his face. Is it not the face of an honest man?" asks a writer in a Cincinnati Republican campaign paper with the same name, whose masthead included the phrase "An honest man's the noblest work of God."

> It bears no marks of deceit, of cunning, of trickery, or demagogism; no marks of duplicity; no evidences which would lead you to think that he would prove false to the great and fundamental truths upon which this Government was formed, or that he would not do justice to all parts of Union. Moderation, sincerity, and moral integrity are . . . written on that homely face of his. . . . How is it that he obtained that proud sobriquet, freely accorded upon all hands and by those who know him best, and which is not a new thing, but by which he has

been familiarly called for years, that of *"Honest Abe Lincoln?"* What better evidence of his *honesty* than this?—one of the proudest appellations that any man could wish: for "An honest man," remember, "is the noblest work of God."

In a later issue of the same publication, in an editorial entitled "Honest 'Old Abe,'" a writer responded to partisan attacks on Lincoln's integrity by stating that "No amount of slander and detraction can ever rob Abraham Lincoln of this well-earned title." Lincoln's honesty was featured in many campaign songs, including *Honest Old Abe* and *Harrah for Lincoln*, the latter contrasting the Republican candidate's unblemished reputation with the besmirched record of President Buchanan.

> A corrupt administration
> Shall no more disgrace our nation;
> Rogues shall seek their proper station,
> For we've found an honest man.
> One with arm that's true and steady—
> One with heart and voice that's ready.
> Yes, good Abraham has said he
> Would consent to lead the van.[6]

It is the homespun, rugged, rail-splitter image and all that it symbolized that one encounters frequently in various forms of print in the months between Lincoln's nomination in May and the November election. Lincoln is presented as a plain, self-made man from the West, an unpretentious man of the people from the frontier who triumphed over adversity through dauntless will and perseverance; a man of impeccable character possessing both moral and physical strength; a man of profound conviction, ingrained integrity, and innate rather than school-learned intelligence; a tireless advocate for free labor; and a faithful disciple of democracy and defender of the Union against the despotism of the slaveholding aristocracy. In short, the Republican candidate and the region from which he hails symbolize America's bold and exciting future. An early issue of Chicago's *The Rail Splitter* contains the poem "Old Abe of the West," which refers to Lincoln's Western upbringing that conferred upon him the self-reliance and strength of character that enabled him to overcome his humble beginnings and to reach the "brow of the hill" while fighting for and representing free labor and free men.

> Our leader is one who, with conquerless will,
> Has climb'd from the base to the brow of the hill;
> Undaunted in peril, unwavering in strife,
> He has fought the good fight in the Battle of Life;
> And we trust him as one who, come woe or come weal,
> Is as firm as a rock and as true as the steel,
> Right loyal and brave, with no stain on his crest,
> Then, hurrah boys, for honest Old Abe of the West!
> And fling out your banner, the old starry banner,
> The signal of triumph for Abe of the West![7]

One Republican campaign song, "The Wood-Chopper of the West," uses the rail-splitter image as a trope to convey the message of Lincoln the pioneer Westerner who will save the country from the evils of greed and slavery.

> And his Herculean arms will hew
> The shadowing trees that hide the view
> Of the grand White House from the West,
> That all may see our eagle's nest.
>
> This woodman is a pioneer
> And he will cut a pathway clear
> From Illinois to Washington,
> Before his noble task is done.
>
> Fence out the wrong of power and place;
> Fence in the rights of all the race;
> Fence out the greedy hand that steals;
> Fence in the noble heart that feels.
>
> Fence out the tyrant and his sway;
> Fence in the hero of the day;
> Fence out oppression, vice, and crime;
> Fence in the truth from heaven sublime.[8]

The image of Lincoln presented in a poem dedicated to the Wide-Awakes, semi-military pro-Lincoln clubs comprised primarily of young men that sprang up during the 1860 campaign, serves as a reminder of the belief that a common man of the frontier, far removed from the world of privilege, can, through hard work, iron will, and smarts, rise above adversity to lead the nation to greatness.

> Once more—if some youth who may list to my song,
> Guides an unwieldy flat-boat the river along,
> Or sweats, like a Trojan at splitting of rails,
> And braves, like a hero, adversity's gales;—
> Who always is true to the dictates of right;
> With no guilt of conscience to haunt him at night;
> Who modest and truthful, will do what he can
> To overcome evil and elevate man;—
> O, let it console him, if e'er he's deprest [sic]
> To think of the lucky *Old Boy of the West!*[9]

Horace Greeley, editor of the pro-Lincoln *New York Daily Tribune* with weekly circulation figures of more than 215,000, avidly emphasized the rail-splitter image. Within days of Lincoln's nomination as the Republican candidate for president, Greeley's daily edition of the *Tribune* asserted that Lincoln combines the "intellectual powers of a giant with the simple habits of a backwoods farmer," possessing that "genuine whole-souled manliness of a Kentucky-born, Western raised, self-educated, and self-made man," who will be "hugged to the people's hearts like a second Andrew Jackson."[10]

Greeley's comparison of Lincoln's son of the soil, self-made man image to that of Jackson is surprising coming from a former devout Whig who found little to like about the former president. Yet his linking of Lincoln with Jackson was, in some respects, apt in terms of both praise and criticism. Concerning the latter, Jackson's opponents portrayed him as an illiterate, immoral, and reckless military chieftain lacking the skills and temperament to be president. Lincoln, of course, could not be accused of adultery and bigamy as was Jackson, although Democrats were quick to denounce his vulgar stories and off-color jokes as coarse and undignified. And unlike Jackson's opponents, Democrats could not label Lincoln a cold-blooded murderer for executing twenty wrongly accused deserters. But Democrats did mock Lincoln's "no battles, no captures" Black Hawk War record. His opponents, especially those Democrats old enough to remember the Whig's successful linking of an image to a candidate in the 1840 Log Cabin campaign, were quick to point out that Lincoln's experience as a common man who split rails and floated a flat-bottom boat down the Mississippi, no matter how attractive the story, did not qualify him to be president. In reality, Lincoln was illiterate, uncouth, lacked any substantial accomplishment in politics, and never held any positions of leadership. In short, according to the Manchester, New Hampshire's *Union Democrat*, the "third-rate western lawyer . . . who cannot speak good grammar" lacked the qualifications to lead the United States.[11]

An article appearing in the Democratic-leaning *Philadelphia Evening Journal* is representative of the arguments used by Lincoln's opponents against his rail-splitter image. "It is evident that the 'Republican' newspapers are hard put to it for something to say in favor of Mr. Lincoln," growls the unnamed writer, for his "record as a statesman is a blank. He has done nothing whatever in an executive, judicial or legislative capacity." Furthermore, there "is not in all the history of his life any exhibition of intellectual ability and attainments fitting him for the high and responsible post in Government for which he has been nominated." The writer continues, it "does not by any means follow that because an individual who, beginning life as a flat-boatman and wood-chopper, raises himself to the position of a respectable County Lawyer . . . [he] is therefore qualified to be president of the United States." "There is," after all, "no fitness or proportion between the two things—between the measure of merit or title and the high and arduous trust to be conferred."[12]

This view echoes that expressed by the *Boston Semi-Weekly Courier*, a newspaper that supported the Constitutional Union ticket of John Bell and Edward Everett. "This is really too ridiculous," responded the editors on May 21, 1860, to the news of Lincoln's nomination at the Republican convention. The editors saw "no reason whatever" for his nomination, "except that he resides in the West—which is a very slim account indeed to give of the candidate." The least the country could expect from the Republicans "was to bring forward a statesman. . . . But the name of Mr. Lincoln awakens neither interest nor respect. To the majority of the people he is altogether unknown, and there is nothing about him to be made known, which can excite any ardor for his cause." Lincoln is "a lawyer far below the highest rank; a partisan, not a statesman; and as a member of Congress formerly, making very little figure and enjoying no marked reputation."[13]

A Boston newspaper with a Republican allegiance saw Lincoln's nomination in a different light. The editors of the *Boston Daily Advertiser* celebrated the party's choice of a plain-speaking Westerner to head the ticket. "The West has now made a nomination from among its own sons," they proclaimed enthusiastically. The Republicans chose a man "full of vigorous life, rough, earnest and practical, rousing in his behalf the deepest enthusiasm among simple people who are around him, attaching them to himself most of all by the frankness of his character and the unblemished honesty of his whole career." Lincoln's nickname "Honest Old Abe" might sound strange to Eastern ears, the editors admitted, but "it conveys a tribute to personal worth, such as is not ordinarily given to men in political life."[14]

The editors of Republican newspapers and other supporters of Lincoln were prepared for attacks on his scant political record and, especially, his unsophisticated Western image. Responding to the *Philadelphia Evening Journal*'s dismissal of Lincoln as presidential timber, Horace Greeley in the June 24, 1860, edition of the *New York Daily Tribune* advances six reasons for supporting the Republican candidate, including Lincoln's long record of political success in Illinois, traditionally a strong Democratic state; his "gradual and steady" rise from "a flat-boatman, a rail-splitter, a farm-hand and a store clerk" to a successful legislator, lawyer, and leader of Illinois's Whig and Republican parties; his election as the only Illinois Whig to the U.S. Congress in 1846 with the largest majority ever given in his district to any candidate running against Democrats, "much larger than any other of which we have a record"; and his 1858 debates against Douglas. "Of Mr. Lincoln's merits as 'a flat-boatman and mauler of rails,' we have little to say," avers Greeley, for we are "no judge of flat-boat navigation; but the rails made by Lincoln thirty years ago, which we saw in Chicago, seemed a very fair article." Nonetheless, men should judge Lincoln "solely by his intellectual and political record as a public man. If the facts do not represent him very different from what *The Journal* represents him, the American People will so decide. We fearlessly await their verdict."[15] In October, weeks before the election, Greeley reinforces the case for his candidate: "It is undeniably true that splitting rails never qualified a man for the Presidency—so let that point be deemed settled," asserts the editor. But Lincoln's case was different.

> Abraham Lincoln illustrates our position and enforces our argument. His career proves our doctrine sound. He is Republicanism embodied and exemplified. Born in the very humblest White stratum of society, reared in poverty, earning his own livelihood from a tender age by the rudest and least recompensed labor, soon aiding to support his widowed mother and her younger children, picking up his education as he might by the evening firelight of rude log cabins, clearing off primeval forests, splitting rails at so much per thousand, running a flatboat, and so working his way gradually upward to knowledge, capacity, esteem, influence, competence, until he stands to-day the all but elected President of this great, free People—his life is an invincible attestation of the superiority of Free People, as his election will be its crowning triumph. That he split rails is of itself nothing; that a man who at twenty was splitting rails for a bare living is at fifty the chosen head of the greatest and most intelligent party in the land, soon to be the Head also of the Nation—this is much, is everything.[16]

Editorials, articles, pamphlets, and campaign newspapers that promoted—or mocked—the rail-splitter image were complemented by scores of publications, including lithographs and engravings issued by commercial firms seeking profits rather than partisan advantage. Broadsides, prints, sheet music, and cartoons were produced with images depicting split rails and flatboats, symbols of the rugged pioneer life. *The Lincoln Quick Step*, sheet music published by the Philadelphia firm of Lee and Walker, featured a portrait of Lincoln surrounded by images of the candidate mauling rails, implements used in rail splitting, poles used by flat boatmen, and a flatboat on a river. The cover of *The "Wigwam" Grand March*, issued by Oliver Ditson in Boston, included, in addition to a portrait of Lincoln, a small drawing of a young man, presumably the candidate, chopping wood.[17]

Sheet music cover for Charles Grobe's composition *Lincoln Quick Step* (Philadelphia: Lee & Walker, 1860). In addition to the portrait of Lincoln, the cover lithographs show Lincoln splitting rails and crewing a flatboat and various implements he would have used in those pursuits. Courtesy of the John Hay Library, Brown University.

Soon after Lincoln's nomination, an Illinois newspaper announced the sale—twenty-five cents each and eight dollars for one hundred—of "a spirited engraving printed in four colors, representing 'OLD ABE, THE RAILSPLITTER,' at his work MAULING RAILS. Flatboat on the left, Steamboat, Farm House and Landscape in the distance, Ox team hauling rails, etc. In the foreground is Abe, Splitting Rails (good likeness), dinner basket, dog, and a copy of 'Blackstone's Law Commentaries' . . . this is a document every Republican should have in his possession." If this print was ever published, no copy of it has survived. Many others were, however, including a Chicago-produced broadside entitled *The Republican Standard*, which includes not only a portrait and brief biography of Lincoln but also a wood engraving of him steering a flatboat on the Mississippi River. New York printmaker H. H. Lloyd's broadside entitled the *National Republican Chart/Presidential Campaign, 1860* features woodcuts of Lincoln and the Republican vice presidential nominee Hannibal Hamlin "IN A VIGNETTE OF LOG RAILS engraved expressly for it."[18]

The Last Rail Split by "Honest Old Abe," a cartoon that appeared in the June 2, 1860, issue of the weekly comic paper *Momus* depicts the Republican candidate "splitting" the Democratic Party in two.[19] Whereas this cartoon presents Lincoln in a positive light, there were scores of others that used the rail-splitter image against him. Currier and Ives, which produced several prints favorable to Lincoln, issued several cartoons that must have warmed the hearts of Lincoln's opponents. One lithograph, *The Rail Candidate*, portrays Lincoln uneasily straddling a split rail depicting the Republican platform that is carried by a black man, presumably representing a freed slave, and Horace Greeley. The cartoon, with its racist overtones, has the Republican candidate bemoaning his awkward situation: "It is true I have Split Rails, but I begin to feel as if *this* Rail would split me, it's the hardest stick I ever straddled." A blatantly racist cartoon that appeared during the 1860 campaign, *"The Nigger" in the Woodpile*, also turns the rail-splitter image against Lincoln. This lithograph depicts the Republican candidate sitting on top of a pile of split rails that represents the party's platform and conceals an enslaved black man. Lincoln remarks that "Little did I think when I split these rails that they would be the means of electing me to my present position." The cartoon shows Greeley standing nearby assuring a man identified as "Young America" that the Republican ticket has "no connection with the Abolitionist party," as "our Platform is composed of rails, split by our Candidate."[20]

Paper cover of *Republican Songs for the People*, compiled by Thomas Drew (Boston: Thayer & Eldredge, 1860). Lincoln's portrait is surrounded by a split-rail fence and images of Lincoln splitting rails and steering a flatboat. Courtesy of Jonathan H. Mann and the Rail Splitter.

* * *

Most Americans who encountered the various genres of print discussed above would have linked Lincoln to the West, a log cabin birth, split rails, and even flatboating, but may not have understood completely the larger context of the symbols' meaning. After all, when Lincoln was nominated in May of 1860—he was not considered a strong contender by many political observers, including some of his own supporters—he was unknown to the vast majority of Americans outside of Illinois, including the author of an early campaign biography who thought Lincoln's first name was "Abram."[21]

For many Americans, Lincoln's biography was virtually a blank slate. This was not, of course, a situation confined solely to Lincoln. In the absence of mass communications, most nineteenth-century presidential candidates, with the exception of war heroes, were unknown to a large segment of the population. This could be seen, in some circumstances, as an advantage, especially for a candidate with an unremarkable life story and an undistinguished record because it presented an opportunity for a candidate's managers or party operatives to create a compelling biographical narrative or embellish a mediocre political record, crafting images and devising symbols to enhance a candidate's attractiveness in the eyes of voters. Thus a candidate's image and the symbols used to promote that image were intertwined with the candidate's life story, no matter how ordinary or mundane; an image by itself might not be enough to resonate with voters, but a life *without* an image might seem to lack meaning or relevance to many. It was in the published campaign biography that a candidate's life story and image were merged with the purpose of introducing him, promoting his candidacy, and convincing readers to vote for him.

Nineteenth-century Americans seeking information about presidential candidates had at their disposal various genres of printed matter. Whereas pamphlets, broadsides, prints, and newspaper articles and editorials offered snapshots of a candidate's life and career, or his views on a particular issue, campaign biographies provided in one place the most extensive amount of information concerning a candidate's life, character, and qualifications for the presidency. The genre emerged during the 1824 presidential campaign waged between Andrew Jackson and John Quincy Adams. John Henry Eaton's 1824 *Life of Andrew Jackson*, a reissue of John Reid's 1817 account of the general's life that he completed, is considered the first presidential campaign biography. Every American presidential campaign since that bitter contest, including those of recent memory in which the autobiography, television, film, the internet, and social media have played increasingly influential roles, has had its share of published candidate biographies.[22]

The purpose of these biographies was to present a positive portrait of a candidate, one that would resonate with voters. Promoting presidential candidates through published biographies—as well as through public events and other genres of print—was especially critical in Lincoln's time because of the accepted tradition of presidential candidates disavowing interest in or openly seeking public office. Thus promotion of candidates was left to the political parties, partisan newspapers and their editors, and nonpartisan publishers and other commercial firms taking advantage of the public's sudden interest in the lives of men who might be president. Generally composed by anonymous party hacks, inexperienced journalists, or budding writers, campaign biographies were presented as being objective and free of partisanship—offering only "facts" culled from interviews with friends, published speeches, or the public record. Authors tended to present themselves as nonpartisan admirers of the candidate, bringing an edifying and inspiring story to the attention of the public out of patriotic duty. Although campaign biographies were essentially propaganda pieces, this does not mean that their contents were invented or inaccurate, though often unflattering aspects or embarrassing episodes were downplayed or omitted. Candidates sometimes initiated and/or participated in private with the production of these biographies. This was, to some extent, the case with Lincoln.[23]

One aspect of presidential campaign biographies that is worth noting is the haste in which they were written and published. With the exception of those that were revisions of previously published works, like Eaton's 1824 account of Jackson, campaign biographies were produced in a matter of weeks in order to be printed, distributed, and, it was hoped, influence as many voters as possible in a limited amount of time. A biography could not be written without a candidate, and who that would be could not be identified until party caucuses or nominating conventions chose a standard bearer. There were, of course, biographies issued before caucuses and conventions took place in order to bolster a certain candidate's chances, but this was the exception rather than the rule. With at most six months between the nomination process and the election, the time for research, writing, printing, advertising, and distribution was indeed short. Lincoln, for example, was nominated on May 18, 1860, approximately six months before the election. This meant that an interested publisher had to choose an author to research and write a biographical account of the candidate, then advertise, print, and distribute the book in a matter of weeks to keep out in front of the competition. This was an enormous undertaking when dealing with a subject who, like Lincoln, was relatively unknown. In many cases, the first campaign biography to appear served as the chief source, with parts thereof often plagiarized for subsequent biographies. This meant that biographies appearing later in a campaign were, in many ways, exercises in duplication and repetition, with readers encountering the same anecdotes, stories, quotes, and speeches.[24]

Campaign biographies ranged in length from a six- to eight-page pamphlet to a three-hundred-page book and in price from twenty-five to fifty cents for a work bound in paper wrappers to one dollar for a cloth-bound edition. Some biographies, including some of Lincoln, were no more than a full-page newspaper article. What is hard to discern is how these biographies were distributed and sold; in other words, how they got into the hands of voters. W. Burlie Brown, whose 1960 work is a useful introduction to the genre, claims that many campaign biographies were not intended for mass distribution. He provides no evidence to back up this assertion, however. Furthermore, he states that "the preponderance of evidence indicates that they were given away, but probably only to active campaigners, for the number of copies purchased by parties seems small." Again, Brown is vague when it comes to evidence, but his statement might be true in instances in which a party either issued the biography or paid for a commercial publisher to do so. This scenario would make sense when parties were not seeking profits through sales but were focused on winning elections. Sending complimentary copies to local party headquarters for distribution at barbecues, parades, rallies, and party gatherings ensured circulation. For example, five thousand copies of Nathaniel Hawthorne's biography of Democratic candidate Franklin Pierce were distributed free in New York City and many more were probably given away in other cities and towns. The Whigs, according to a prominent party insider, were doing the same for Pierce's opponent, General Winfield Scott, distributing "about a million" copies of his campaign biography.[25]

One finds it hard to believe that nonpartisan publishing houses would follow this practice of dispensing large quantities of complimentary copies of candidate biographies unless the works were subsidized by one of the political parties or by a group of supporters. In fact, Brown himself suggests the probability that "a much larger number of campaign lives came into the hands of the voters through their own purchases." Unfortunately, sales figures of the period are virtually nonexistent. Yet, as Brown points out, existing evidence for the nineteenth century, albeit meager, indicates "a fairly brisk trade." According to one Chicago bookseller, sales of John C. Frémont's biographies reached seven thousand in 1856. Ticknor and Fields, the publisher of Hawthorne's 1852 *Life of Franklin Pierce*, printed over fifty thousand copies of Charles Wentworth Upham's campaign biography of Frémont four years later, obviously expecting active sales. Brown cites an estimate of "certainly 100,000 and possibly as many of 200,000 copies of Lincoln's biographies" were distributed during the 1860 campaign. It is not known, however, exactly what he means by *distributed*, nor if he is referring to all of Lincoln's biographies or merely some of them. Nevertheless, Brown is probably right when he claims that publishers expected heavy sales not only from the general public but also from political parties making bulk purchases with the intention of distributing complimentary copies. Virtually every publisher of campaign biographies offered cheap editions and discounts for bulk ordering. In 1840, the publishers of two campaign biographies of Whig William Henry Harrison offered one at a discount of $1.80 per dozen, $13.50 per hundred, and $120 per thousand, and the other at $6 per hundred, $48 per thousand, and $425 per ten thousand. Discounts such as these, directed to booksellers and to political parties and organizations, were common during the nineteenth century. Within weeks of the 1852 elections, Ticknor, Reed, and Fields was selling Hawthorne's biography of Franklin Pierce at a 40 percent discount to entice booksellers to submit bulk orders.[26]

When it came time to prepare campaign biographies of Lincoln, authors did not have far to look for models, for by 1860 there were four decades worth of similar works to consult. Nineteenth-century presidential campaign biographies adhered to a fairly consistent formula, both in terms of structure and content. For one thing, many contained a woodcut or engraved image or images of the candidate, providing readers a chance, especially in the days before photography and the ability of newspapers to print illustrations, to see what a particular candidate looked like. If a candidate's reputation rested on his military exploits, as was the case with William Henry Harrison, Zachary Taylor, and Winfield Scott, his biography might include one or more woodcuts depicting his participation in famous battles.[27] Sometimes these accounts contained, along with the life story, a selection of letters and speeches of the candidate, as well as a short biography of the vice presidential nominee. It was in the section devoted to the candidate's letters and speeches that political issues pertinent to the campaign—and the candidate's opinions concerning these issues—were usually presented. The biographical section tended to concentrate on a candidate's life story, downplaying or, in some instances, ignoring completely partisan politics.

To understand presidential campaign biographies and their contents, they must be examined within the broader context of the evolving genre of biography in nineteenth-century America. Biography was an extremely popular genre during this century, beginning with the post–Revolutionary War period. There were debates early in the century over how much of a subject's "domestic privacies" or private life should be explored, with many observers claiming that a subject's *public* life was a better reflection of his character. During the 1830s, biographies began to discuss their subjects' private lives, a gradual shift that became increasingly apparent in campaign biographies published since that time.[28]

By the time of Lincoln's first campaign for the presidency, there was general agreement among writers concerning the purpose of biographies—presenting a life that would both inspire and instruct. In other words, biographies offering readers lives worth emulating—lives devoted to the common good and rising above the boisterous and sometimes undignified world of politics. This recurring image, presented in a series of episodes in one's life, is shaped by certain factors considered essential to the makeup of a virtuous and moral life, including one's ancestry; parents; early life; education; military experience; farming, business, or political career; domestic and private life; and religious beliefs.[29]

A candidate's ancestry receives much attention in these works, with authors seeking to establish a noble lineage for their subject: a descendent not from aristocracy or great wealth but from forebears who resisted Old World tyranny in the name of religious and political liberty. A candidate directly linked to ancestors who participated in the American War of Independence had an advantage over a candidate who lacked such a lineage.[30]

Despite the importance of parents or guardians to inculcate the values that guide future candidates (such as morality, good character, and patriotic citizenship), they receive little attention in early nineteenth-century campaign biographies, though one notices a gradual shift to more inclusion after midcentury. Parental roles are established in the earliest biographies, however. Candidates' fathers are depicted as passing on such virtues as patriotism, responsible citizenship, integrity, charity, and hard work. Fathers, whether poor or financially successful, tend to be portrayed as industrious, honest, and respected members of their communities. Mothers, on the other hand, overseeing the domestic environment in which future candidates are raised, are celebrated for shaping their offspring's moral and religious character. In their different ways, both parents are seen to be responsible for instilling the civic and moral values of patriotic citizenship.[31]

Details of a candidate's childhood and adolescent years receive little attention in campaign biographies published before the 1850s.

Although a gradual shift in coverage of candidates' early years begins to appear around midcentury, it is not until after the Civil War that these formative years receive any serious attention. When describing their subject's childhood and adolescent years, antebellum presidential campaign biographies tend to replicate the model inspired by the imagination of Mason Locke Weems, whose portrayal of George Washington's boyhood devoid of lies and mischief was as shamelessly unbelievable as it was extremely influential.

The education of candidates is discussed in most campaign biographies, regardless of how much formal schooling they received. Those who had the advantage of a formal education at some level are always presented as above average or as exceptional students, especially drawn to the subject of history. No matter how successful future candidates are in the classroom, however, they are never portrayed as academic intellectuals devoid of practical common sense. Candidates deprived of a formal education due to humble circumstances make up for this deficiency by following a disciplined regimen of self-education. But whether self-taught or having the advantage of formal schooling, candidates are described as practical men who use book learning for utilitarian purposes. Proud, ambitious, and popular with their peers, these men overcame modest or humble environments—many were born in log cabins or simple cottages—in which they were raised and achieved success as a result of hard work, innate ability, and dauntless ambition. In other words, they are self-made men.[32]

Military experience, especially if it included valor on the battlefield, garners more attention in nineteenth-century campaign biographies than any other aspect of a candidate's life. The volunteer, or citizen-soldier, is often presented as following in the footsteps of George Washington, who, more than any other American, embodied the image of the self-sacrificing patriot who lays aside his plow and leaves his home and family to fight for his country. Any candidate who demonstrated bravery in combat and leadership on the battlefield held a distinct advantage over an opponent who lacked such experience. It is not surprising that the military exploits of Andrew Jackson, William Henry Harrison, Zachary Taylor, and Winfield Scott dominate their campaign biographies. The message communicated by these works and of others like them is that leadership in war is an excellent preparation for leadership in civilian life.[33]

For many candidates, however, it is what they accomplish in their civilian life—in addition to or instead of military service—that prepares them for the presidency. In nineteenth-century campaign biographies, candidates are presented either as sturdy yeoman farmers or as successful businessmen. While few candidates focused their careers solely on agriculture, many did possess a connection with farming at some point in their lives. However tenuous the candidate's relationship to the soil might have been, it is nevertheless exploited in order to link the candidate to the traditional republican ideal of the sturdy yeoman farmer as a virtuous advocate of democracy. Among those candidates who did not make their living via the plow, many practiced law. But whether they were farmers, businessmen, or lawyers, all candidates are portrayed as ambitious without being greedy or ruthless, successful but not wealthy, and as leaders but not "bosses" of their communities.[34]

A candidate's political career receives almost as much attention in campaign biographies as his military exploits. After all, a politician creates a record that documents his stands on the various issues of interest to voters. As mentioned above, many campaign biographies included a selection of a candidate's speeches, letters, and publications so that voters could familiarize themselves with a candidate's record. No matter how long and distinguished a candidate's political career might be, however, their campaign biographer made a concerted effort to assure readers that he is not a professional politician, but rather a reluctant public servant who, under pressure from the people, serves his country in the halls of government. In other words, the office seeks the man rather than the other way around. Candidates tend to be portrayed as nonpartisan patriots operating in a cesspool of chicanery and corruption, serving the cause of good government, standing for principles over partisanship, and representing the people rather than any one party.[35]

Minimal space is devoted to candidates' private or domestic lives and religious views in nineteenth-century campaign biographies.

What is written about these matters falls into a fairly consistent pattern, however. Candidates are presented as leading pure and moral lives. Their private habits, like their homes, are pious and unpretentious. A candidate's wife and children receive little attention. All candidates believe in god, are deeply religious, are orthodox Christians, and ardent advocates of religious freedom. Most attend church on a regular basis.[36]

The most common virtues attributed to candidates in nineteenth-century presidential campaign biographies are benevolence, industry, integrity, honesty, humility, morality, and piety. All are described as men of strong character, as inspiring leaders, and as true patriots. W. Burlie Brown put it best when summing up the virtues of presidential candidates as portrayed in campaign biographies:

> And so they have been simple republicans all. Plain men, scorning fashion, forthright in speech, unpretentious in manner. As American as apple pie, outwardly they are indistinguishable from the man next door. They live comfortably on their modest means, loving their simple homes, enjoying the good fortune of a wife who is equally at home behind the kitchen stove or in the public eye, delighting in their children and those of their neighbors, worshipping God with deep but unostentatious piety, and behaving in a manner that is approved by the moral sense of their community.[37]

As the reader will discover in the upcoming chapter, Lincoln's campaign biographies did not diverge from the model described above. In some respects, Lincoln's 1860 biographies had to address areas in which he could be perceived as weak or vulnerable, including his scant military record, his controversial religious views, and his meager political experience on the national stage. One thing these biographers had working for them, however, was an attractive image that emerged from the Illinois Republican convention. Their task was to craft a biography to fit the image.

CHAPTER THREE

PROMOTING HONEST ABE, THE
RAIL SPLITTER: LINCOLN'S 1860
CAMPAIGN BIOGRAPHIES

Perhaps Abraham Lincoln truly believed that there was "not much of me" for a biography of more than a few pages in length. Several publishers and the authors they commissioned, however, thought otherwise. According to one source, within a day of Lincoln's nomination on May 18 at least six publishers announced forthcoming campaign biographies of the rail-splitting candidate. Eight days after Lincoln's nomination, a Republican newspaper in Erie, Pennsylvania, the *True American*, claimed there were four publishing houses with biographies in the works.

> There will soon be no lack of biographies of "Honest Old Abe" in the market, as well as no lack of readers to welcome them! W. A. Townsend & Co. will soon publish a life of our candidate with a steel portrait in a dollar volume, and a campaign edition for 25 cts. H. Dayton will issue about the 10th of June a biography with a portrait. Derby & Jackson will publish immediately another "Life" written by Bartlett, the Washington correspondent of the New York Evening Post, and Follett, Foster & Co. of Columbus, Ohio, are about to undertake a similar publication.[1]

As a Republican organ, the *True American* either received advertisements directly from publishers planning to issue Lincoln campaign biographies or its editor encountered such advertisements in other

Republican newspapers received through an exchange network. As it turned out, the newspaper's source or sources only grazed the surface concerning plans for Lincoln biographies. This chapter will show that the publishers cited by the *True American* would soon be joined by several others interested in producing accounts of Lincoln's life. By the time of Lincoln's election, sixteen campaign biographies—a few in several editions and two issued only in German and Welsh—were published, with all but one appearing within a matter of weeks after Lincoln's nomination. Lincoln's 1860 biographies almost equal the number issued for his three opponents combined. These works, as was the case with biographies promoting Lincoln's rivals, were issued in pamphlet or book form, bound in paper wrappers or cloth bindings, ranging in price from twenty-five to fifty cents for the paper versions to one dollar for the cloth editions, and, in most cases, included a wood or steel engraving or a woodcut of the candidate.[2]

The authors of the earliest campaign biographies used Joseph Lewis's February 1860 *Chester County Times* account as the basis for their works. The first biographical account after the May Republican convention appeared in the *Chicago Press and Tribune* on May 19, the day after Lincoln's nomination. Probably written—in haste—by John Locke Scripps, the multipage article was published on the same day in several Eastern newspapers, including Horace Greeley's *New York Daily Tribune*, and in the May 26 edition of *Harper's Weekly*, which featured a woodcut of Lincoln based on a photograph taken at Mathew Brady's New York studio when Lincoln was there in February to give his Cooper Union speech. Despite working from the same article, some versions, including the *Harper's Weekly* piece, got Lincoln's first name wrong, referring to him as "Abram," indicating just how little known he was to the Eastern press, not to mention Eastern readers.[3]

Not all biographical material presented in every Lincoln campaign life was borrowed directly from Lewis or other early accounts. Soon after Lincoln's nomination, publishers' agents and biographers either traveled to Springfield to interview the candidate and those who knew him or wrote to him seeking details of his life. While Lincoln made every effort to meet with writers, journalists, artists, and photographers, he could not keep up with the mail from those wanting biographical information. As a result, his secretary John G. Nicolay prepared a generic letter that was used to respond to such requests:

> Dear Sir:
> Your letter to Mr. Lincoln of _____ by which you ask his assistance in getting up a biographical sketch of him is received. Applications of this class are so numerous that it is simply impossible for him to attend to them.[4]

Several campaign biographies were issued in early June 1860. It appears that *The Life, Speeches, and Public Services of Abram Lincoln*, published by the nonpartisan New York firm Rudd and Carleton, was the first book-length biographical account of the Republican nominee. Rudd and Carleton, publishers of American literary works and translations of popular French authors, was one of several firms that announced on May 19 that a Lincoln biography was "in press." Published on June 2 and called "The Wigwam Edition" in reference to the temporary structure in Chicago in which Lincoln was nominated, this work used either the May 19 sketches or the May 26 *Harper's Weekly* version, as well as the Lewis biography, as the bases for its narrative. Bearing a woodcut image derived from the Cooper Union photograph on its paper cover, this biography, like many others that followed in its wake, also includes speeches of Lincoln and a brief account of the life of vice presidential candidate Hannibal Hamlin. The unknown author (possibly George W. Carleton, who occasionally dabbled in writing) got Lincoln's first name wrong, which may be attributable to the haste with which the work was assembled from the earlier *Harper's Weekly* sketch—mistakes and all. The sales of *The Life, Speeches, and Public Services of Abram Lincoln* were strong: twenty thousand copies in its first month on the market. With several variants issued in Lancaster, Pennsylvania, Portland, Maine, Springfield, Massachusetts, Providence, Rhode Island, and Chicago, this work was one of the most popular Lincoln campaign biographies.[5]

One Lincoln biographer was David W. Bartlett (1828–1912), a journalist for the *Springfield (Mass.) Republican*, Washington correspondent for the *New York Evening Post*, and the author of several books, including an 1852 campaign biography for Democratic presidential candidate Franklin Pierce. Bartlett was commissioned by either Derby and Jackson or H. Dayton, both New York City publishers, to write a campaign biography of Lincoln. Presumably working together, both firms announced on May 19 their intention of publishing campaign biographies of "Abram" Lincoln. Two days later their advertisements were reissued with the candidate's correct first name. On June 4, Bartlett's *The Life and Public Services of Hon. Abraham Lincoln* was published by H. Dayton, with a variant issued on the same day by Derby and Jackson, which appeared to be a politically neutral enterprise. Published in paper covers with an engraving of Lincoln based on the Cooper Union photograph, Bartlett's work covers Lincoln's life, along with excerpts of his speeches and letters. Omitting biographical material on Hannibal Hamlin, this is the first biography in book form devoted solely to Lincoln. Bartlett's work is based heavily on—even using exact phrases from—the *Chicago Press and Tribune* article and the Lewis sketch. A second revised edition, also issued in paper and falsely stating that it was an "Authorized Edition" (no campaign biographies were authorized by Lincoln), was published about two weeks later, with the plagiarized passages deleted or changed.[6]

Since clothbound books took longer to publish, the earliest campaign biographies to reach the market appeared in paper wrappers. Both H. Dayton and Derby and Jackson issued cloth editions of Bartlett's work on June 12, with a steel engraving of Lincoln's Cooper Union photograph as the frontispiece, and including additional speeches of Lincoln as well as a biographical sketch of Hamlin. A second cloth edition also was published, sometime in early July, with variants issued in New York, Cincinnati, Philadelphia, and Indianapolis.[7]

The short-lived (1859–61) Radical Republican Boston firm of Thayer and Eldridge announced in the May 19 edition of the *Boston Transcript* that a Lincoln biography was forthcoming. What the firm did not advertise was that it had banked on William Seward being nominated at the Republican convention and thus had been about to publish a biography of the New York senator, written anonymously by the London-born antislavery advocate Richard Josiah Hinton

Cover of *The Life, Speeches, and Public Services of Abram Lincoln* (New York: Rudd & Carleton, 1860), the first book-length account of Lincoln's life to be published after his nomination at the Republican National Convention. Courtesy of the John Hay Library, Brown University.

(1830–1901). Like the New York publishing houses of Rudd and Carleton, H. Dayton, and Derby and Jackson, the Boston firm moved quickly to produce the Lincoln biography, announcing it was "on hand" on June 7. Written anonymously (because of his known ties to John Brown) and in haste by Hinton, *The Life and Public Services of Hon. Abraham Lincoln, of Illinois, and Hon. Hannibal Hamlin, of Maine* was published within days of the appearance of the Seward biography. Issued in paper wrappers with woodcut portraits of both Lincoln and Hamlin, this work, like its predecessors, relied heavily on the *Chicago Press and Tribune* article as well as on the Lincoln-Douglas debates that Lincoln arranged to be published earlier in 1860. A second edition soon appeared, and in late June an expanded version of this work, cloth-bound and labeled the "Wide-Awake Edition," was issued with an additional two hundred pages devoted to speeches.[8]

Several brief Lincoln biographies were published at the end of May and early June 1860. One, an eight-page pamphlet of a May 29, 1860, speech delivered in the U.S. House of Representatives by Lincoln's close friend from Illinois, Elihu Washburne (1816–87), was published by the Republican Congressional Committee. Washburne's *Abraham Lincoln, His Personal History and Public Record* offers a short and partisan account of the candidate's life and includes the Republican Party's platform. Published within a week or two after the congressman's speech, the pamphlet sold for fifty cents per hundred (and was probably given away for free at parades and rallies). This biographical sketch relied heavily not only on the *Chicago Press and Tribune* article but also on the congressman's long association with the candidate. Admitting to Lincoln that the pamphlet was "hastily got up," Washburne quoted liberally from his colleague's speeches, defending his friend's record in Congress, particularly emphasizing Lincoln's votes in support of supplies for soldiers fighting in the Mexican War despite his opposition to the conflict.[9]

Another brief campaign account of Lincoln was written by Ichabod Codding (1810–66). Born in Bristol, New York, Codding was a Congregationalist minister and ardent abolitionist who lectured on the subject across the Northeast and West and established antislavery newspapers in Maine and Connecticut. Spending time in Illinois, where he was involved in founding the state's Republican Party, Codding came to know Lincoln and attempted, without success, to push Lincoln into the abolitionists' camp. His ninety-six-page *A Republican Manual for the Campaign*, issued sometime during the first two weeks in June of 1860, contains a brief six-page biography of Lincoln—a complete reprint of the *Chicago Press and Tribune* article. Codding used this publication to solicit support among Republicans for the abolitionist cause and to apologize for what he considered Lincoln's conservative views on the abolition of slavery. Due to the scarcity of this work (less than ten copies are known to exist), one scholar believes that the Republican Party suppressed it because of the radical views expressed by the author.[10]

Almost as scarce on today's market is Reuben Vose's *The Life and Speeches of Abraham Lincoln and Hannibal Hamlin*, which was published—in paper wrappers for fifteen cents—in New York by the author about the same time as Codding's and Washburne's biographies. The bulk of the book is comprised of Lincoln's speeches, with his biography, based heavily on the *Chicago Press and Tribune* article (except for the glaring error that claimed Lincoln's father died when the candidate was a young boy), appearing in the first 6½ pages of the 118-page work. The book's scarcity could be the result of Vose failing to attract agents to sell the work.[11]

One of the several publishers announcing a forthcoming campaign biography the day after Lincoln's nomination was Follett, Foster, and Company of Columbus, Ohio, the same firm that issued the Lincoln-Douglas debates. Not only did the publishing house announce its intention of producing an account of the Republican nominee's life, but one of its representatives telegraphed Lincoln, requesting that he "please designate your pleasure if any as to who the writer shall be." There is no evidence that Lincoln ever responded. The publisher soon commissioned William Dean Howells (1837–1920), a twenty-three-year-old associate editor of the *Ohio State Journal* who performed occasional hackwork for the firm, to travel to Springfield, Illinois, to interview Lincoln, his friends, and associates, using the material gathered to write a biography.[12]

Although Howells agreed to write the biography, he found the idea of traveling to Springfield "distasteful," believing he had "nothing of the interviewer in me."[13] Thus the task was left to James Quay Howard, a twenty-year-old law student in Columbus, Ohio, whom Howells hired to collect material for the book. During Howard's brief visit to Springfield he was treated cordially by Lincoln, who shared a biographical sketch he had prepared for Scripps, and by Lincoln's secretary John G. Nicolay, who assisted him in assembling biographical data. Howard returned to Columbus apparently believing that Lincoln had authorized Howells's work. But when Follett, Foster, and Company advertised the first edition of the biography as "Authorized by Mr. Lincoln," the firm received a swift and terse response from Springfield. In a June 15 letter to the publisher, Nicolay claimed that the firm's assertions were "very wrong," and that neither "Mr. Lincoln nor myself ever said or did anything, which could give Mr. Howard or yourselves any reason to suppose you had such 'authority.'" Asking the firm to "recall your announcements," Nicolay stressed that Lincoln "neither *authorizes* yours or any other biography of himself." On June 19 Nicolay sent Howard a similar letter, in which he reiterated that Lincoln "cannot '*authorize*' '*endorse*' or '*be responsible for*' the book." In a letter to an associate, Lincoln claimed to be "astounded" by Follett, Foster, and Company's claim, retorting that "I *authorize nothing*—will be *responsible* for *nothing*." The publishers quickly changed the wording of its advertisements to read "accurate and reliable."[14]

As it turned out, Howells used little of Howard's research, relying instead on previously published biographies, especially Hinton's. Howells's *Lives and Speeches of Abraham Lincoln and Hannibal Hamlin* was published—his name did not appear on the title page—in paper wrappers on June 25. The 170-page book, written quickly and rushed into print, includes an engraved portrait of the candidate based on the Cooper Union photograph. Lincoln later read this version of Howells's biography and made several minor corrections, though the author claimed he never saw Lincoln's emendations.[15] On July 5 a second edition, cloth bound, was issued, this time with Howells listed on the title page as author. It contains more than four hundred pages, including six additional Lincoln speeches and more information on the Chicago convention, as well as biographical information on and speeches by Hamlin contributed by John L. Hayes.

Cover of the first edition of William Dean Howells's *Life of Abraham Lincoln* (Columbus, Ohio: Follett, Foster & Co., 1860). Courtesy of the John Hay Library, Brown University.

Several variants of this edition were published in Cincinnati, Boston, Chicago, Detroit, and New York, which may indicate its popularity.[16] Howells was later appointed by President Lincoln to the post of consul to Venice.[17]

"Before the meeting of the Republican National Convention of 1860 I had undertaken, not of my own motion or at first willingly, to write a campaign biography of its nominee for the Presidency." So writes Joseph Hartwell Barrett (1824–1910), editor of the *Cincinnati Daily Gazette,* delegate to the 1860 Republican convention, and the author of the *Life of Abraham Lincoln,* published in a paper-cover version in late June and in hard-cover in early July by the prominent Cincinnati firm of Moore, Wilstach, Keys, and Company. Comprising more than two hundred pages, Barrett's work included a lithograph of Lincoln based on a photograph commissioned by the author, a selection of Lincoln's speeches, and a biographical sketch of Hannibal Hamlin. A variant of this work was issued in Indianapolis. In addition to relying on previously published biographies, Barrett also gathered information directly from Lincoln during at least two visits to Springfield, as well as from works on Kentucky and Indiana history. He subsequently developed a friendship with Lincoln, who appointed him U.S. Commissioner of Pensions in 1861. As will be discussed in the next chapter, Barrett also wrote an 1864 campaign biography of the president.[18]

The autobiographical sketch that Lincoln had shared with Howard in Springfield was his second attempt at writing a brief account of his life and career. The first, written for Jesse Fell, embellished by Joseph Lewis, and published in the *Chester County Times* early in 1860, was used by several early biographies, including Scripps's May 19 *Chicago Press and Tribune* account. Scripps wanted to write a fuller account of the candidate's life, however, and requested further biographical details from his friend. Lincoln, according to Scripps, was reluctant to cooperate, claiming that "it is a great piece of folly to attempt to make anything out of my early life. It can all be condensed into a single sentence, and that sentence you will find in Gray's Elegy: 'The short and simple annals of the poor.' That's my life, and that's all you or any one else can make of it."[19] Lincoln soon relented, however, and sometime in June sent Scripps a longer version (nine short paragraphs written in the third person) of what he had prepared for Fell months before.[20]

Working quickly to compete with other campaign biographies already on the market, Scripps drafted a ninety-six page account of Lincoln's life, expanding on what he had written in his earlier sketch. His manuscript was reduced to sixty pages at the direction of Horace Greeley, his New York publisher, which resulted in significant cuts in the final section, virtually ending the work with the 1858 Lincoln-Douglas debates. Furthermore, due to time constraints, Scripps did not submit the manuscript for Lincoln's approval as he had promised. He later apologized to the candidate for the "sadly botched" final section and for not giving him a chance to review the draft.[21] Scripps's *Life of Abraham Lincoln*, published simultaneously by the *Chicago Press and Tribune* and Horace Greeley's *New York Daily Tribune* (as *Tribune Tracts, No. 6*), appeared around July 15 as a thirty-two page, double-column pamphlet. A second Chicago edition was subsequently issued.[22]

Although he had informed Lincoln that he had added "nothing that I was not fully authorized to put into it," Scripps freely embellished Lincoln's manuscript, adding details concerning his ancestors, parents, and religious upbringing that the candidate chose to omit. One item that came solely from Scripps's imagination concerned Lincoln's reading of *Plutarch's Lives*, a book Lincoln never mentioned in his sketch. Without checking with Lincoln, Scripps claimed that the candidate had read the work: "What fields of thought its perusal opened up to the stripling, what hopes were excited in his youthful breast, what worthy models of probity, of justice, of honor, and of devotion to great principles he resolved to pattern after, can be readily imagined by those who are familiar with his subsequent career." Scripps told Lincoln that if he had not already read *Plutarch's Lives*, he "must read it at once to make my statement good." Evidently, Scripps's biography was popular, for more than one million copies were sold. After assuming the presidency, Lincoln appointed Scripps postmaster of Chicago.[23]

Despite having published the Lincoln-Douglas debates and Howells's campaign biography, Follett, Foster, and Company produced another work about Lincoln for the election season. Since little of the material Howard assembled for Howells's work was used, the publishing house or Howard came up with the idea of producing another campaign biography. Howard's *The Life of Abraham Lincoln: With Extracts from His Speeches* was published in late July 1860. Appearing in paper wrappers, this publication, unlike several other campaign biographies, did not include a section on the life of Hannibal Hamlin. Knowing that the election was generating great interest in the local German community, Follett, Foster, and Company issued a German-language edition of this work. Howard was later appointed U.S. Consul at St. Johns, New Brunswick by President Lincoln.[24]

In addition to the works devoted to Lincoln mentioned above, there were four other biographical treatments that appeared in larger works published prior to the November election. The *Republican "Campaign" Text-Book for the Year 1860*, written by the composer, music critic, and journalist William Henry Fry (1813–64) and published by A. B. Burdick in New York City, includes brief sketches of Lincoln and Hamlin that consist of only one page in the 108-page book.[25] Whereas Fry's book was directed to Republican loyalists or those voters leaning toward the party, there were three other works published for a much wider audience, including independent, uncommitted, or undecided voters. New York City publisher J. G. Wells's *Illustrated National Campaign Hand-Book for 1860*, for example, in addition to offering a concise political history of the United States, features biographical sketches and engraved images of each presidential and vice presidential candidate. Issued simultaneously in New York and Cincinnati in two parts, Wells's handbook is a lavish production compared to many of the other 1860 campaign publications. The Lincoln biographical chapter, accompanied by a woodcut image of the candidate based on the Cooper Union photograph and including copious extracts from his speeches, covers twenty pages.[26]

It is not known how soon after the nominating conventions that Wells's book was published or who wrote the biographical sketches of Lincoln and the other candidates. One suspects that Wells commissioned hack writers (or wrote the sketches himself) to prepare brief biographical accounts based on material that had already been published. This was probably the case with two other similar works, *The Lives of the Present Candidates for President and Vice President of the United States* and *Portraits and Sketches of the Lives of All the Candidates for the Presidency and Vice-Presidency, for 1860*. The former, published simultaneously in paper wrappers in Cincinnati, Philadelphia, St. Louis, and Geneva, New York, contained the platforms of the Republican, Democratic, and Constitutional Union parties in addition to biographical accounts of the candidates. Lincoln's biography, including a crude woodcut of the candidate based on a photograph taken in either Peoria or Springfield around 1858, comprises 28 of the book's 139 pages.[27] The New York engraver J. C. Buttre produced a handsome pamphlet in paper wrappers of portraits and sketches of the 1860 candidates. Lincoln's section of the 32-page work consists of a 2-page biographical account along with a steel engraving based on the ubiquitous Cooper Union photograph.[28]

Biographers of the 1860 presidential candidates, as has been mentioned, had little time—a matter of weeks—to prepare accounts of their subjects' lives. One suspects that the task was somewhat easier for those writing biographies of Douglas, Breckinridge, and Bell due to their extensive public records. This, of course, was not the case with Lincoln, an obscure Western politician in the eyes of many outside of Illinois. Moreover, despite his keen understanding of the political advantages of his rustic Western image, Lincoln was extremely reluctant to dwell on it. After all, he spent most of his adult life distancing himself from his humble beginnings and the physical drudgery associated with clearing forests, building cabins, splitting rails, and farm work. Yet, it was this very image of the rough-hewn Western, rail-splitting candidate that fired imaginations and generated enthusiasm for Lincoln's campaign. Moreover, it provided a frame on which campaign biographers could build a compelling life story.

Selected biographers, of course, had at their disposal Lincoln's autobiographical sketches, as well as information he shared during interviews. This material, however, provided very little grist for the proverbial mill; thus biographers were forced to look elsewhere for material—from Lincoln's friends, associates, and acquaintances, other published Lincoln biographies, or their own imaginations. For the most part, Lincoln's biographers followed the model of previous presidential campaign narratives, crafting a positive account of the candidate's life, emphasizing his numerous qualities and strengths that prepared him to serve as president of the United States.

Like most presidential campaign biographies, Lincoln's usually began with mention of the candidate's lineage. Lincoln himself revealed little concerning his ancestry, due primarily to the simple fact that he knew almost nothing about his parents' forebears. He claimed that his grandfather and father emigrated from Virginia to Kentucky and were descended from Quakers in Pennsylvania. But, as he wrote in the brief autobiography he prepared for Jesse Fell, efforts to connect his ancestors "with the New England family of the same name ended in nothing more definite, than a similarity of Christian names in both families."[29] Lincoln's ignorance concerning his ancestral line did not stop an early biographer from asserting that the candidate "has revolutionary blood in his veins," linking him with the Lincolns of Massachusetts, "known for their patriotism in the war of '76." The most famous of the Massachusetts Lincolns was the Revolutionary War general Benjamin Lincoln, who served under George Washington at Yorktown.[30] Vose and Barrett also link the candidate with the Massachusetts Lincolns, though Barrett qualifies his assertion, claiming that "one tradition indeed affirms that the Pennsylvania branch was transplanted from Hingham, Mass., and was derived from a common stock with Colonel Benjamin Lincoln, of Revolutionary fame."[31]

Later campaign biographers are more cautious when discussing Lincoln's connection to revolutionary forebears. Howells goes no further than to suggest that the link is "a dim possibility." The biographical sketch in J. G. Wells's *Illustrated National Campaign Hand-Book* contends that Lincoln "is probably descended from the Lincolns of Massachusetts," while the anonymous author of the Lincoln biography in the *Lives of the Present Candidates for President and Vice President* claims nothing more than "speculations are afloat as to the identity of the branch from which he sprung."[32] While some biographers were unwilling to establish Lincoln's ties to an ancestral line gilded by association with the American Revolution, all confidently assert connections to solid Pennsylvania and Virginia stock. Hinton's biography pronounces that Lincoln descended from "good old stock by whom the State of Pennsylvania was founded," while J. Q. Howard avows that the candidate's forebears, both maternal and paternal, were distinguished "for honesty and industry."[33]

Lincoln in his autobiographical statements is less than forthcoming about his parents. What little Lincoln says about his father in the brief sketch he sent to Scripps is dismissive: that he "grew up literally without education" and never did more in the way of writing "than to bunglingly sign his own name." Lincoln lost his mother, Nancy Hanks Lincoln, when he was nine years of age and undoubtedly felt a profound sense of loss. He nevertheless developed a loving relationship with his stepmother, Sarah Johnston, whom his father married a year after Lincoln's mother's death, writing that she "proved a good and kind mother."[34]

A candidate's parents receive scant attention in early nineteenth-century presidential campaign biographies. This began to change around midcentury, with coverage becoming more pronounced after the Civil War. Thus Lincoln's campaign biographies appeared during a time of transition concerning the treatment of parents. Faced with a candidate reluctant to open up about his father, mother, and stepmother, Lincoln's biographers tend to merge the stories of his parents into a larger account of the hardscrabble life and impoverished circumstances of his youth. While Lincoln may have been self-conscious when it came to the lowly status of his parents and his own humble beginnings, his campaign biographers showed no such reluctance. What Lincoln was reticent to discuss (but made no attempts to suppress), his biographers were eager to exploit as essential props and scenery for a rags-to-riches story full of struggle, heartbreak, and backbreaking work. Lincoln's upbringing by "poor and uneducated" parents in a harsh, primitive environment was presented not as an indictment but as a moral lesson of what one could achieve through hard work, perseverance, and true grit.[35] Every biographer describes the candidate's youth as one of meager subsistence. Barely making ends meet, the Lincoln family moved from Kentucky, where Abraham was born, to Indiana, where he spent most of his youth, from one rustic log cabin to another, sometimes with seven or eight living in one room with a loft. Finally, Thomas Lincoln settled his family down in Illinois. Life was hard for young Lincoln, who endured the deaths of his mother, a younger brother, and an older sister.

Lincoln's frontier upbringing with almost no access to educational opportunities was far from unique; it was an experience shared by many of his generation, especially those born in the West and South.[36] Yet Lincoln's campaign biographies celebrate his triumph over the seemingly insurmountable obstacles faced by those Americans struggling to tame the wild frontier in a typically American way, with hard work, an iron will, and a burning ambition to learn and to improve his station in life. Howells emphasizes Lincoln's ability wielding an axe: "until he was twenty-three, the ax was seldom out" of the candidate's hand, "except in the interval of labor, or when it was exchanged for the plow, the hoe, or the sickle." "At the early age of nine," writes Howard, Lincoln "began his life of toil, earning his bread by the sweat of his brow, at the severest physical labor. The axe was the first weapon he wielded." Despite its iconic association with Lincoln, the axe was not the only implement of labor he employed. According to Scripps, Lincoln was constantly "engaged in the various kinds of labor incident to the country and the times—felling the forest, clearing the ground of the undergrowth and of logs, splitting rails, pulling the cross-cut and the whip-saw, driving the frower, plowing, harrowing, planting, hoeing, harvesting, assisting at house-raisings, log-rollings and corn huskings," while "mingling cordially with the simple-minded, honest people with whom his lot was cast."[37]

The privations and the backbreaking work associated with pioneer life instilled in Lincoln "an honorable conscientiousness, integrity, industry, and an ardent love of knowledge," as well as "a restless ambition" to improve himself and achieve success in a chosen calling.[38] Virtually all biographers mention Lincoln's two flatboat trips to New Orleans, which involved not only hard work requiring physical stamina, but a strong dose of courage. Not surprisingly, his rail-splitting exploits are highlighted. Elihu Washburne was one of several biographers who mention Lincoln's first year in Illinois when he split "three thousand rails." In the words of Howard, the rail splitting candidate, helping his father build a log cabin and clear land for farming, split enough rails "to fence ten acres of ground." It is these very rails, he declares, "about which so much has been said, and so much enthusiasm manifested."[39]

Lincoln's prowess with an axe, his flatboat experiences, and his years of incessant toil on the family farm are not presented merely to showcase his physical strength (which biographers mention admiringly) or his work ethic. Rather, campaign biographers seek to communicate a broader message, that of Lincoln as a friend of ordinary people and, especially, the common laborer. Lincoln passed from boyhood to manhood, contends Scripps, "in full sympathy with the people, rejoicing in their simple joys and pleasures" and "united with them all by that band of brotherhood among the honest poor—a common heritage of labor." For Lincoln, Barrett declares, the dignity of labor "became . . . a true and appreciable reality." Because he was accustomed to a life of steady labor, "no one of all the working-men with whom he came in contact was a better sample of his class than he."[40]

Nineteenth- and early twentieth-century homespun images of the young Lincoln reading by the hearth fire in the family's rustic log cabin may be romanticized, but there was a real story behind the sentimentality, a story that many campaign biographers eagerly sought to convey. Lincoln's lack of formal education—his attendance at school amounted to less than a year—is emphasized in all the 1860 biographical accounts. Yet, despite the fact that he "barely received the rudimentary elements of a common English education," writes one biographer, he lost no opportunity "to cultivate his mind."[41] That he did not grow up illiterate was the result of hard work, a disciplined regimen of self-education that built upon an innate intelligence, a profound thirst for knowledge, and a burning ambition to succeed in life. Readers of Barrett's biography learn that Lincoln is "chiefly a self-educated man," who, as a youth "read with avidity such instructive works as he could obtain, and in the winter evenings, by the mere light of the blazing fireplace, when no better resource was at hand."

According to Howard, Lincoln "read everything within his reach." And his self-education was not confined to his youth; he continued to cultivate his mind after he left home and settled in New Salem, where "he felt the need of a more thorough knowledge of text-books." Determined to master English grammar, Lincoln, unable to obtain a copy of Kirkham's *Grammar* in the immediate vicinity, "walked about seven miles and borrowed an old copy." Lincoln not only learned the fundamentals of grammar, adds Scripps, but "at twenty-five he mastered enough geometry, trigonometry, and mensuration to enable him take the field as a surveyor." Moreover, Lincoln "studied the six books of Euclid after he had served a term in Congress."[42]

Lincoln's early life was not restricted solely to work and book learning, however. Despite his love of reading, he was not a book-worm. He loved the outdoors, athletic activities, and knew how to have fun. Lincoln's popularity among his peers is one aspect of his youth and his New Salem years that all biographers underscore. Anecdotes and stories demonstrating his physical strength, courage, and sense of humor are encountered in most of the 1860 campaign biographies as evidence of his ability to attract friends and, later, followers. According to Scripps, Lincoln as a young man evinced "social qualities which rendered his companionship desirable; remarkable even then for a wonderful gift of relating anecdotes, and for a talent of interspersing them with acute and apt reflections." He was "everywhere a favorite, always simple, genial, truthful, and unpretending, and always chosen umpire on occasions calling for the exercise of sound judgment and inflexible impartiality." "It is scarcely necessary," Scripps avers, "to add that he greatly excelled in all those homely feats of strength, agility, and endurance, practiced by frontier people in his sphere of life."[43]

No incident in Lincoln's early life exemplified his courage and physical strength more than his famous wrestling match with the notorious Clary Grove Boys. Led by Jack Armstrong, considered the strongest man and best wrestler in the New Salem region, the clan was known for its rowdy behavior and for terrorizing people in the town and surrounding countryside. When the boys heard of the strength and wrestling prowess of the tall, lanky newcomer

Lincoln, they challenged him to a wrestling match with their leader Armstrong. Many of the campaign biographers either recount or at least mention the match, which is presented as a key turning point in Lincoln's life. As Howard describes it, in Lincoln, the Clary Grove Boys thought they had found a pushover. But it did not take Armstrong long to realize that "he had got hold of the wrong customer." While the match ended in a draw, Lincoln "completely won their hearts by his courage and bravery." Howells echoes Howard, avowing that "Lincoln's fearless conduct had already won the hearts of his enemies. He was invited to become one of their company. His popularity was assured."[44]

Unlike many of the successful presidential candidates that preceded him, such as Andrew Jackson, William Henry Harrison, and Zachary Taylor, Lincoln had scant military experience. Having little to work with, Lincoln's biographers emphasize his patriotism and his popularity with his peers. All stress Lincoln's patriotic response to the call for volunteers during the Black Hawk War and his election by an overwhelming vote as captain of his militia unit, which included several of the Clary Grove Boys. Moreover, when his company was disbanded, Lincoln revolunteered and served as a private in another unit. Despite the fact that he never engaged in combat, he is praised by his biographers for his service to his country. One applauds Lincoln for "serving gallantly in the Black Hawk War of 1832," while another commends the candidate for acquitting himself "with credit."[45] Others expand on these brief acknowledgements, including Barrett, who opines that Lincoln "faithfully discharged his duty to his country, as a soldier, persevering amid peculiar hardships, and against the influence of older men around him, during these three months' service of this his first and last military campaign." An anonymous biographer contends that Lincoln "proved himself 'every inch a soldier.' In all the privations of camp, in all the marchings, counter-marchings, over marshes, through 'the trembling ground' . . . under every step of the soldier, he observed the daily routine which approved himself a man, and endeared him to his comrades."[46]

While there were no heroic battlefield exploits to tout, there was one incident in Lincoln's Black Hawk War experience that several biographers cite as an example, in the words of Howard, of his "kind heartedness, magnanimity and bravery." When an elderly Indian wandered into Lincoln's camp bearing a pass signed by a U.S. government official, several of Lincoln's men wanted to kill him. Declaring that such an action against a friendly, unarmed Indian was a barbaric act, Lincoln faced a potential revolt in his unit. Responding forcefully to charges of cowardice, he challenged anyone to take him on, announcing that if they wanted to kill the Indian, "they must do it over his dead body."[47]

Although Lincoln spent his first twenty years on a farm, his relationship to the soil ended when he left his family to strike out on his own. Detesting farm work, Lincoln had no intention of pursuing a career in farming. Unable to link the candidate to the noble calling of tilling the land, his biographers concentrate their efforts on his various jobs as flat boatman, store clerk and store owner, surveyor, postmaster, and lawyer. Readers discover that Lincoln participated in two flatboat trips to New Orleans, endeavors known for "exposure . . . hard labor, and of constant peril," so much so, that they, according to Scripps, "developed and nurtured a race of men peculiar for courage, Herculean strength, hardihood, and great contempt of danger." During Lincoln's first trip in 1828, he and his fellow boatman were attacked in the middle of the night by a group of black men intent on robbing the boat of its goods. The "would-be robbers and assassins," affirms Scripps, had not "properly estimated the courage and prowess" of Lincoln and his companion, who gave the attackers "a warm reception, and, notwithstanding the disparity in numbers, after a severe struggle, in which the two boatman were considerably hurt," drove them from the craft. Lincoln as flat boatman was almost as compelling an image as those of rail splitter and "Honest Abe."[48]

Lincoln's honesty is demonstrated by two incidents included in almost every biographical account. The first involves a biography of George Washington, which a young Lincoln had borrowed from a neighbor. The book was damaged by water while in Lincoln's possession and the boy, not having the money to replace the work, vowed to the owner that he would work off his debt. He did so in three days. The second example of Lincoln's integrity relates to his short-lived career as a store owner in New Salem. In 1832, he entered into a partnership with William F. Berry to operate a grocery store. Having little capital, the owners went into debt buying merchandise on credit. This debt was exacerbated a year later when the co-owners purchased the stock of another store. Berry's heavy drinking, however, resulted in Lincoln breaking up the partnership, selling his share to the unreliable Berry. When Berry's store, in the words of Lincoln, "winked out," suits were filed against both Berry and Lincoln for unpaid debts.[49] When Berry died, Lincoln assumed all the store's remaining debts, totaling more than one thousand dollars. Though it took him several years, forcing him to sell most of his personal belongings in the process, Lincoln paid the debt in full. Lincoln's last installment was paid from his first earnings as a practicing lawyer. The moral of this episode, avers Howells, "need not be insisted on" because it is "not out of the order of Abraham Lincoln's whole life. That old neighbors and friends of such a man should regard him with affection and faith little short of man-worship, is the logical result of a life singularly pure, and an integrity without flaw."[50]

Despite Lincoln's success as a lawyer and the integral role it played in his life, his legal career, surprisingly, receives minimal coverage. This is due, perhaps, to nineteenth-century Americans' distrust of the legal profession. Nevertheless, Lincoln's rapid rise in the profession is noted, with Scripps declaring that Lincoln "obtained a reputation at the bar which placed him in the front ranks of the many able and profound jurists" of Illinois. Bartlett reminds readers that while Lincoln was virtually self-taught in the law, he nevertheless quickly gained distinction as a master of persuading juries through well-crafted presentations that were "master-pieces of logical reasoning," bearing the "stamp of masculine common sense." Readers of Howells's work learn that Lincoln would never "undertake a cause which he believed was founded in wrong and injustice."[51]

When reviewing Lincoln's legal career, biographers emphasize that he is self-taught, honest, and he defends the common man. Several cite the famous "almanac" trial as an example of Lincoln's integrity, kindness, and willingness to fight for a good cause and a poor client. The case involved the son of the late Jack Armstrong, who was involved in a fight in which he was accused of murdering one of the participants. The case appeared to be open and shut against the accused. Moreover, the defendant's mother could not afford to hire a lawyer. Lincoln volunteered to take on the case as a friend of the family. Making use of an almanac, which contradicted key testimony for the prosecution that there was a full moon on the night of the murder, Lincoln convinced the jury to render a verdict favorable to the young Armstrong. When Armstrong's widow attempted to pay him what little she had, Lincoln refused to accept remuneration for his work. Hinton's biography includes an excerpt from the *Cleveland Leader* account of the case that runs four pages in length. Barrett devotes four pages to the trial, and Howells describes the courtroom saga in a long note. "Lincoln, who seems to have believed firmly in the young man's innocence, volunteered in his defense, and in throwing aside the well-connected links of circumstantial evidence against him, made the most touching and eloquent appeal to the sympathies of the jury.... Young Armstrong was acquitted; and Lincoln refused to accept any reward for his defense."[52]

Lincoln's political career, as meager as it was, receives more attention from his biographers than any other aspect of his life. Most review his four terms as a state legislator, his one term on Congress, and, especially, his debates with Douglas in the 1858 U.S. Senate race in Illinois. Concerning his state assembly and congressional careers, Lincoln's biographers describe him as a consistent Henry Clay Whig, a strong advocate of the "American System" of federal support for internal improvements and a protective tariff. Lincoln, claims Barrett, believed deeply in the duty of government "to extend its fostering aid, in every Constitutional way, and to a reasonable extent, to whatever enterprise of public utility required such assistance, ... to the fullest development of the natural resources, and to the most rapid healthful growth of the State."[53]

Congressman Lincoln is portrayed as an ardent opponent of the Mexican War, though all biographers, fully cognizant of the possible negative political impact of this stance, stress his support of the troops when he served in the House of Representatives. Scripps asserts that "Mr. Lincoln voted in favor of every measure of this kind which came before Congress." Barrett denounces Lincoln's Democratic opponents for "unscrupulously" conflating his opposition to the war to include hostility to the troops while he was "voting supplies and for suitable rewarding our gallant soldiers."[54] As the war drew to a close, the issue of allowing slavery into territory acquired from Mexico emerged as an issue in Congress. Lincoln's fervent support of the Wilmot Proviso and his eloquent advocacy of free labor in the territories are highlighted by his biographers. But many of them emphasize that Lincoln is not an abolitionist. Rather he is presented as a man of moderate views on slavery—morally opposed to the institution and its extension into the territories but convinced that the federal government was prevented by the Constitution from abolishing slavery where it already existed. According to Hinton, Lincoln "belongs by character and association to that school of moderate, conservative men, who sought the peaceful extinction of slavery." In Bartlett's view, Lincoln is "a cautious, conservative reformer" when it comes to the slavery issue.[55] In his pre-Republican days, Lincoln is portrayed as a popular, honest representative of the people, and, in the words of Barrett, "as one of the soundest and most effective of Whig champions in the West."[56]

Several biographers point to the passage of the Kansas-Nebraska Act of 1854 as a transformative event in Lincoln's political career. This controversial legislation, which Hinton refers to as the offspring of "the scheming ambitions of an unscrupulous aspirant to the Presidency" and another calls an "outrage perpetrated by the Democratic Party," repealed the Missouri Compromise and set the stage for epic battles between the act's author, Stephen Douglas, and Lincoln, first as a leader of the Illinois anti-Nebraska forces, then as a rival for Douglas's senate seat in 1858, and finally as candidate for president two years later.[57] In his famous debates with Douglas, Lincoln is portrayed as his rival's equal in debating skills and superior in his cause, or, in the words of Barrett, "an able statesman, an effective orator, a true gentleman, and an honest man." Bartlett devotes one whole chapter to the debates, while many of the biographies include excerpts of Lincoln's remarks, especially those delivered at Freeport where he forced his opponent to defend popular sovereignty against the

Supreme Court's Dred Scott decision, thus alienating many Southern Democrats. Biographers lament that although Lincoln won the popular vote, he lost the election in the legislature due to "fraudulent districting" by Democrats.[58] In summing up Lincoln's political career, his biographers point to his superb performance in the debates, his eloquence on the stump, his ability to connect with the people of Illinois, his reputation for honesty and integrity, his long-standing support of workingmen and free labor, and his courage to fight for the right no matter the political costs as critical factors leading to his nomination as the Republican nominee for the presidency.

Lincoln's domestic and private life, in keeping with the tradition set by previous campaign biographies, receives scant attention. Lincoln revealed very little about his private life in the two biographical accounts he composed. Lewis's early 1860 account, based on information Lincoln gave to Jesse Fell, describes the Republican candidate as a "strictly moral and temperate man." Although Lincoln was a teetotaler and avoided tobacco, practices many of his campaign biographers applaud, his biographers tended to exaggerate moral virtues. Howard praises Lincoln's personal habits as "most abstemious." His food "is plain, and his drink is cold water. He is a man of purest morals. He never drank a drop of liquor; never uses tobacco, and was never guilty of a licentious act. He never uses profane language, and never gambles." Of course, no mention is made in any biographical account of Lincoln's well-known propensity for telling smutty stories and coarse jokes.[59]

Lincoln is presented as a prosperous and successful, but not wealthy, man of plain rather than ostentatious tastes. "At home," Lincoln "lives like a gentleman of modest means and simple tastes," writes Bartlett. Howells affirms that those who visit Lincoln at his Springfield, Illinois, home "are pleased no less at the simple and quiet style in which he lives, than at the perfect ease and cordiality with which they are received." His residence "is a comfortable two-story frame house" with its surrounding grounds "neatly and tastefully kept." The candidate's domestic abode, according to Howard, "is plain and unassuming," like its "distinguished inhabitant."[60]

Lincoln's biographers have little to say about the candidate's family or home life. Several biographical accounts mention Lincoln's three sons and the fact that one had died; in most cases their names and ages are not indicated. Only three biographers, Scripps, Barrett, and Howells, say much about Mary Lincoln, and what they say counters the negative perception of the Lincoln's as unsophisticated hicks. Generally, Mary's treatment by the press at this time was positive, a sharp contrast to the blistering criticism she would face once in the White House. Scripps describes her as "a lady of charming presence, of superior intelligence, of accomplished manners, and in every respect well fitted to adorn the position" of First Lady. "No man," claims Barrett admiringly, "was ever more fortunate in his domestic relations than Mr. Lincoln has been; the accomplished manners and social tastes of his wife, which make her a general favorite, being not less conspicuous than her devotion to her family, and her care to render their home cheerful and happy, as well as cordially hospitable to all." Howells informs readers that Mary Todd, at the time of her marriage to Lincoln, was "the belle of Springfield society—accomplished and intellectual, and possessing all the social graces native in the women of Kentucky."[61]

As pointed out in the previous chapter, early nineteenth-century presidential campaign biographies rarely discuss a candidate's religion or religious views. This certainly was the case with the 1860 Lincoln biographies, a distinct advantage for the candidate since he was known to hold unorthodox views concerning Christianity. It was well known—and publicly admitted by Lincoln—that he was not a member of any church. When he ran for Congress in 1846, questions were raised by Lincoln's opponents about his adherence to Christian doctrine, forcing him to issue a handbill in which he defended himself against charges that he was an "open scoffer at Christianity."[62] Several biographers assure readers that Lincoln regularly attends church and knows his Bible. "He is a regular attendant upon religious worship," confirms Bartlett, and "though not a communicant, is a pew-holder and liberal supporter of the Presbyterian Church, in Springfield, to which Mrs. Lincoln belongs." Scripps argues that there are few men in public life as "familiar with the Scripture as Mr. Lincoln." Howard confirms that Lincoln "has by his means and influence always been a supporter of Christianity."[63]

* * *

The image of Lincoln promoted by his 1860 campaign biographies is that of a man extraordinarily successful in life despite facing seemingly insurmountable barriers. He is portrayed as a leader of men and as a statesman capable of guiding the nation through the storm forming on the horizon. Despite being raised by illiterate parents in a hostile and primitive frontier environment, suffering the emotional traumas associated with pioneer life, and denied formal schooling, Lincoln became, through hard work, perseverance, clean living, and a tenacious regimen of self-improvement, "Honest Abe," the "Rail Splitter," the ideal self-made man. To Lincoln's biographers, his nicknames symbolize something much deeper than integrity and the ability to wield an axe and a maul; they personify the noblest aspects of the American character. In short, Lincoln is a representative American. "Men of experience and culture and training in the arts of polished life have claimed the highest honors in America as abroad," writes one biographer, but the "natural result of democratic institutions is now accomplished," and the Republican Party "has selected for its standard bearer, one who never received more than six months' schooling, who has not only sprung directly from the people, but who still belongs to the people, who is one of them, and among them." Lincoln is "a legitimate result of democracy . . . in his history and in his character is the true offspring of a democracy."[64]

Another biographer refers to Lincoln as "a representative man," not only "of the early Western stock, the hunter, farmer, and pioneer, but an admirable example of what energy and ability can do for a man honestly using them in honorable pursuits." In character and in person, Lincoln is "a type of the West." In Scripps's opinion, Lincoln rightly deserves the appellation of a *self-made man*, for he presents "in his own person the best living illustration of the true dignity of labor, and of the genius of our free American institutions, having been elevated through their instrumentality from poverty and obscurity to his present distinguished position." A man like Lincoln, posits Vose, is destined to lead the nation. After all, the nation's "first and principal task . . . has been to subdue the vast wilderness. . . . This has been our destiny." Western pioneers "have been the instruments of this success . . . and in Abraham Lincoln we behold one of the most hardy and adventurous of these backwoodsmen. A pioneer, a woodcutter, a boatman and a farmer, he has, in each vocation, typified one grand and characteristic mission of our people."[65]

Lincoln's image as a rail splitter and a man of integrity tied him to the American pioneering mission and to the democratic ideals embodied in that noble endeavor. The collective message conveyed by these 1860 campaign biographies is that Lincoln is the right man for the time, a time when the democratic principles and free labor ideology he represented are under siege by a slaveholding aristocracy. His reputation for honesty, however, was extremely relevant in 1860. Several biographers point directly to the allegations of corruption within the Buchanan administration, a major campaign issue for the Republican Party. Barrett compares Lincoln's reputation to that of President James Buchanan: "As a man of the people, in cordial sympathy with the masses . . . as a man of sterling integrity and incorruptible honesty, he is felt to be a suitable agent for rescuing the federal government from its present degradations." Unlike the current occupant of the Executive Mansion, Lincoln's honesty, boasts Howard, "cannot be exaggerated. . . . If elected President, our country will never have had a purer administration."[66]

To Howells, Lincoln's story represents all that is admirable about the American nation; he is not only a man worthy of its highest office but a model worth emulating:

> The purity of his reputation, the greatness and dignity of his ambition, enable every incident of his career, and give significance to all the events of his past. It is true that simply to have mauled rails, and commanded a flat-boat, is not to have performed splendid actions. But the fact that Lincoln has done these things, and has risen above them by his own force, confers a dignity upon them; and the rustic boy, who is to be President in 1900, may well be consoled and encouraged by his labors.[67]

With sixteen campaign biographies, Lincoln was far ahead of his three rivals for the presidency in 1860. Nine biographies promoting

Stephen A. Douglas have been identified along with five for John C. Breckinridge and four for John Bell. These works, like the Lincoln biographies, promote the candidacies of their subjects and craft appealing images for voters. Biographers of Douglas, Breckinridge, and Bell, however, faced an enormous task of fashioning images as attractive as "Honest Abe, the Rail Splitter."

Having sought and lost the Democratic Party's presidential nomination in 1856, Douglas set his sights on 1860 and began to organize a national campaign soon after he defeated Lincoln in the 1858 Illinois senate race. Before the 1860 Democratic convention he opened an unofficial campaign headquarters in New York City and assembled a steering committee. Meanwhile, his Washington office coordinated the printing and distribution of his speeches, supplied friendly newspaper editors with material, and commissioned James W. Sheahan (1824–1883), editor and founder (with the aid of Senator Douglas) of the *Chicago Times,* to write a campaign biography to be ready for distribution at the Democratic convention in Charleston, South Carolina, in late April.[68]

Douglas's plans ran afoul in Charleston, however, where the issue of slavery in the territories engendered a sectional rift among assembled Democrats. Once seen by many as the front runner for the Democratic Party nomination, Douglas alienated many Southern Democrats, not to mention President James Buchanan, as a result of his strong advocacy of popular sovereignty and his fight against the admission of Kansas under the pro-slavery Lecompton constitution. A number of Southern delegates refused to support the Illinois senator, believing he could not be trusted to protect slavery in the territories. Several Southern delegations favored a federal slave code providing such protection, and when they failed in their quest to incorporate the code into the party platform, they walked out of the convention. The remaining delegates were unable to select a nominee due to the lack of a quorum, forcing them to adjourn and to meet again in Baltimore in mid-June. The break did little to heal the rift between Douglas's supporters and several Southern delegations. When the Baltimore convention opened, Southern delegates who bolted the Charleston convention arrived to find that they had been replaced by delegates pledged to Douglas. Although the Little Giant was nominated, Anti-Douglas Southerners ended up walking out of the Baltimore convention and convened in another part of the city, nominating Vice President John C. Breckinridge of Kentucky as their candidate on a platform espousing a federal slave code. Now split among Northern and Southern wings, the Democratic Party offered the country two presidential candidates in 1860.[69]

The Democratic Party was not only bitterly divided, but its two candidates were late organizing their campaigns against the unified Republican Party, not to mention the newly formed Constitutional Union Party, which posed a real threat to both Douglas and Breckinridge in the Border States. Douglas's campaign, which desperately needed Northern as well as Border State support to have any chance at winning the election, fell behind the Republicans in fundraising, garnering newspapers' support, and producing and distributing campaign material, such as speeches and German language publications. This situation prompted Douglas to break with tradition and actively campaign, thus attracting opprobrium and ridicule.[70]

Sheahan's campaign biography was privately authorized by the campaign; not only did Douglas's people commission him to write it—and he complained about not being paid on time—but Douglas himself participated in the editing process, rewriting several chapters.[71] Published by the prominent New York firm of Harper, Sheahan's book was well advertised. It was joined by several other biographical works, Henry M. Flint's *Life of Stephen A. Douglas, United States Senator from Illinois*, published by Derby and Jackson in New York (a publisher of a Lincoln campaign biography); Robert Bruce Warden's *A Voter's Version of the Life and Character of Stephen Arnold Douglas*, issued by Follett, Foster, and Company (a publisher of two Lincoln campaign biographies as well as a book on the Lincoln-Douglas debates); two pamphlets; and chapters in three general works that covered all four candidates. In addition to these publications, there was one biographical account published in German.[72]

Unlike Lincoln, Douglas was well known to many Americans as a politician on the national scene, a leading Northern Democrat who for almost two decades had served as both a congressman and a senator. Having a public record, of course, was a benefit as well as a curse. Douglas had his share of ardent supporters and implacable enemies, and thus his campaign biographies tend to pursue a dual purpose, that is, to remind potential voters of his many talents and successes while defending his reputation and record.

Douglas's political career, including lengthy extracts from his speeches, dominates the biographies by Sheahan, Flint, and Warden. Yet, readers of these and other works are offered a full account of the candidate's life. The image of Douglas created by his campaign biographies depicts a "Little Giant," a self-made man and a man of the people, one who fights against all odds and many enemies (abolitionists, Republicans, and radical Southern Democrats) for what he believes is right, despite public opinion. "Fathers may point their sons with pride to him as a living example of the results of early application, diligence, industry, and perseverance," touts one biographer. Born poor, "without friends or means, in a then unsettled and semi-barbarous state," Douglas, by sheer determination and intelligence, "worked his way up to the highest places, and distinguished each by the ability he brought to bear in the performance of duty. At this time there is no man in the Union more universally esteemed. He is the idol of the people."[73]

Like Douglas, Vice President Breckinridge got a late start in his presidential quest. He did not begin the year 1860 with any presidential aspirations, but he considered the nomination of the Southern wing of the Democratic Party, in the words of one historian, "the very height of honor." Nevertheless, when the campaign began in earnest, Breckinridge and party managers had to move quickly to build an organization from scratch. Not surprisingly, plans were put into place to produce and disseminate campaign literature in the form of pamphlets of speeches and essays promoting the candidate and the party platform. In addition, a biography was prepared and sympathetic editors, especially those in the North, cultivated.[74]

Of the five Breckinridge campaign biographies, only one appeared to be initiated by his party, "Campaign Document No. 8," a thirty-two page pamphlet that included sketches of the nominee and his running mate, Joseph Lane of Oregon.[75] The remaining four were issued by commercial publishing houses. All were produced in haste and were issued separately as short pamphlets or as chapters in larger works that included biographies of all of the candidates running in 1860.[76]

Breckinridge's greatest strength was in the lower South, but like Douglas, he needed to do well in the Border States to have any chance of winning the presidency or throwing the election into the House of Representatives. This reality undoubtedly shaped the image constructed by his biographers, especially the author commissioned by the National Democratic Executive Committee. Elected vice president in 1856 at the young age of thirty-five, the Kentucky-born Breckinridge rose quickly in politics, a fact noted by all of his biographers. According to one, Breckinridge's career was "one of the most brilliant and successful in the annals of the distinguished men of our country."[77]

Breckinridge's biographers fashioned an image that would appeal to voters in the Border and Northern states. He is portrayed as a disinterested public servant, called to high office to save a nation in crisis. According to his authorized biographer, all the "elements of a great and noble character seemed blended in him—truth, generosity, prudence, judgment, intrepidity, a devoted love of his country."[78] Another biographer contends that he "is a courtly and polished gentleman, chivalrous and high-toned, the very soul of honor . . . a man of intellect, honest and straightforward in the expression of his opinions, no politician, no wire-puller, no trickster, prompt in decision, quick in execution, a very lion in the tribe of Jackson." Breckinridge, his biographers imply, would protect the Union from abolitionists, Republican radicals, and Douglas Democrats bent on tearing it asunder.[79]

In 1860 there were four biographies of John Bell, the Constitutional Union candidate for president, all of which were published by commercial publishers, including Rudd and Carleton, which also issued a Lincoln campaign biography.[80] Bell's campaign biographies, like Breckinridge's, tend to emphasize the man as a politician or statesman, while revealing little about the candidate's personality, personal life, or human side. In contrast to the biographies of Lincoln and Douglas, readers are offered few anecdotes about him.

Bell's biographers promote the candidate's maturity (he was sixty-three-years old), experience, moderation, integrity, judgment, patriotism, and long service to his country. While other candidates were willing to push sectional issues that threatened to divide the nation, Bell, whose prospects depended on winning the Border States, always placed compromise above sectionalism and the Union above party and politics. As one biographer opines, Bell's record is "distinguished by a dignity of character, solidity of argument, and suavity of manner . . . our Republic has had few sons to whom she is more indebted than to the calm, philosophic, dignified statesman of Tennessee."[81]

Lincoln won the 1860 election, garnering 59 percent of the electoral college vote (180 versus 123 for Breckinridge, Bell, and Douglas combined) and carrying eighteen states, all of which were in the North and West, except New Jersey (split with Douglas) and Kentucky (won by Bell). Breckinridge was his closest competitor in the electoral vote count with 72, carrying eleven states. While Lincoln won the electoral vote by a wide margin, he won only 39.8 percent of the popular vote, 1,866,452 votes to 2,813,741 for his three opponents, with Douglas winning 1,375,157, almost half of Bell's and Breckinridge's combined total. As Michael Green points out, Lincoln's popular vote percentage was the smallest received by any president up to that time.[82]

CHAPTER FOUR

THE 1864 CAMPAIGN: THE RAIL SPLITTER AS FATHER ABRAHAM

A divided opposition was certainly a key factor in Lincoln's success in 1860. Facing two Democratic rivals as well as a third-party candidate, however, did not ensure Lincoln's victory. Voters cast their ballots for a variety of reasons, whether out of loyalty to one party or hostility to another, religious beliefs, ethnocultural factors, local issues, or on the advice of or pressure from family and friends. Certainly, a compelling image of a self-made Westerner, a man of the people, and an honest man who will save democracy from corrupt politicians and slaveholding aristocrats, transmitted through campaign biographies and other genres of print, motivated many Northern and Western voters. Would the Lincoln image of 1860 hold up four years later? When Lincoln ran for reelection in 1864, the political landscape had changed dramatically for him and for the nation. The purpose of his 1864 biographical accounts, unlike their 1860 counterparts, was not to introduce Lincoln to American voters, but to endorse the reelection of a president who had led the nation through a long and bloody civil war, issued the Emancipation Proclamation, and withstood vigorous political opposition, including members of his own party.

Both revered and reviled within the Northern states, Lincoln, by the summer of 1864, was in trouble politically. His chances for reelection appeared to be slipping away as the war dragged on and battlefield casualties continued to mount at a shocking rate. The

Copperhead segment of the Democratic Party was gaining the upper hand on its pro-war counterparts, while convincing growing numbers of Northerners that Lincoln was not only waging a vengeful, brutal war on fellow Americans but was shredding the Constitution and abusing the powers of the presidency. As proof, they pointed to the Emancipation Proclamation, the suspension of habeas corpus, conscription, and Lincoln's support of the confiscation of property and slaves of those siding with the Confederacy. As Democratic hopes of defeating Lincoln rose significantly in the summer of 1864, Republicans, even ardent supporters of the president, grew increasingly despondent. Some looked to General Ulysses S. Grant as a possible replacement for Lincoln while a coterie of Radical Republicans and abolitionists nominated General John C. Frémont as their presidential candidate a week before the Republican convention.[1]

Despite doubts concerning his chances at reelection, Lincoln was nominated on the first ballot at the Republican convention, held in Baltimore in early June. His adept use of patronage and shrewd cultivation of the press—awarding printing contracts and government positions to friendly newspapermen—enabled him to maintain enough support within the Republican Party and among War Democrats to fight off the possibility of serious opposition at the convention. Continuing the brilliant strategy begun in 1862 of linking support for Unionism and the war with patriotism, "non-partisan partisanship" as one historian calls it, Lincoln and Republicans adopted the name National Union Party and replaced Vice President Hamlin with War Democrat Andrew Johnson as Lincoln's running mate. At the same time, the party endorsed a constitutional amendment outlawing slavery throughout the nation, an action which dealt a fatal blow to the Frémont campaign.[2]

In late August, the Democrats, with prowar and peace factions battling for control of the convention, met in Chicago to nominate candidates for president and vice president. Mirroring its internal divisions, the party nominated General George B. McClellan, who made clear his intention to end the war on the battlefield by demanding reunion as a precondition for peace talks, while choosing antiwar Democrat from Ohio George H. Pendleton for vice president and adopting a peace platform that called for immediate negotiations to end the war.[3]

Days before Democrats met in Chicago, Lincoln received a bleak assessment regarding his reelection chances from Henry J. Raymond, editor of the *New York Times* and chairman of the Republican/National Union Party Committee. "The tide is setting strongly against us," Raymond reported despondently, and nothing but the "most resolute and decided action, on the part of the Government and its friends, can save the country from falling into hostile hands." Blaming the dark political situation on "the want of military successes" and the "impression in some minds, the fear and suspicion in others, that we are not to have peace in any event under this Administration until Slavery is abandoned," he predicted that a number of key Northern states would forsake the president come November. On August 24, the day after reading Raymond's disheartening account, Lincoln composed a short memorandum and then asked his cabinet to sign, but not read (until after the election), the document which indicated he was resigned to defeat in November: "This morning, as for some days past, it seems exceedingly probable that this Administration will not be re-elected. Then it will be my duty to co-operate with the President elect, as to save the Union between the election and the inauguration; as he will have secured his election on such ground that he cannot possibly save it afterwards."[4]

The mixed message conveyed by the Democrats' choice of a prowar nominee tied to a peace platform espousing an immediate end to the conflict presented the Republicans with a glimmer of light amid dark clouds of despair. These clouds were dispersed and the gloom that permeated the Lincoln reelection campaign was lifted by news of General William Tecumseh Sherman's capture of Atlanta a week after the Democratic convention. Although Lincoln's reelection chances improved significantly in September 1864, supporters of both the president and McClellan engaged in an intense and bitter campaign that had, in reality, begun before the nominating conventions, with each side proclaiming that the future of the country was at stake and the election of the opposing candidate would either result in a dictatorship under a tyrant or in the elevation of a traitor to the presidency.[5]

Although tradition and the heavy responsibilities of managing a war prevented Lincoln from promoting his own reelection, he had many national, state, and local party leaders working on his behalf and friendly editors and journalists mobilizing support. His state papers, speeches, and public letters were put to use in 1864 by his campaign managers, political supporters, and commercial firms to remind voters of where he stood on the issues, his leadership qualities, and his eloquence. The task of Republican Party operatives, as well as commercial firms promoting Lincoln's reelection, was quite different than four years earlier, however, when their candidate was an obscure Western lawyer unknown to many Americans.

The "Honest Abe, the Rail Splitter" image presented to voters in 1860 was, by itself, inadequate four years later. Now well known to most Americans and with a record to defend, Lincoln required no introduction. Moreover, Lincoln's opponents, through vitriolic editorials, fiery speeches, and racially charged cartoons, had been defining him for years as an uncouth hick, an incompetent commander in chief, a tyrant intent on destroying the Constitution and the country, and a rabid abolitionist determined to force racial equality and miscegenation. The "Honest Abe, the Rail Splitter" image was by no means ignored, however. In 1864, this image served as a platform or foundation on which biographers could build a new image appropriate for the time. Thus, the task facing campaign managers, the Republican Party, and other supporters was mounting a vigorous defense of Lincoln's first term as president, reminding voters of his many virtues and his captivating life story, and portraying Democrats as unpatriotic political partisans in time of war and even as traitors to the United States.

As it had in previous elections, print played a dominant role in the presidential campaign of 1864. Broadsides, posters, pamphlets, sheet music, songsters, ballots, cartoons, and newspapers served as channels through which the political parties communicated their messages and mobilized their constituents. Various genres of print were also issued by commercial publishers advocating a certain candidate or cause, or merely seeking financial profit by taking advantage of Americans' interest in the election. As expected, campaign biographies of both Lincoln and McClellan flooded the market in the months preceding the election.

Ten Lincoln biographies were published for the 1864 presidential contest, with nine of these accounts including material on Lincoln's life before his presidency. Two, and possibly four, of these works were issued before Lincoln's official renomination, either signaling confidence or concern about his chances. Many include engraved portraits of the president and excerpts of his letters, speeches, and proclamations. Surprisingly, there were no Lincoln (or McClellan) biographies published in German or Welsh, as there had been in 1860, possibly indicating confidence in the president's popularity with these particular constituencies. In addition, there were two studies of Lincoln based on the pseudo-science of phrenology, as well as two humorous accounts of the candidate's life which appeared to neither advocate nor denounce his reelection.[6]

One of the first 1864 Lincoln campaign biographies to appear was Henry Raymond's *History of the Administration of President Lincoln*, published sometime in May before the National Union Party convention or within days after Lincoln's nomination on June 8. With less than 50 of the 496 pages devoted to Lincoln's life before 1860, Raymond's book was intended to place the president's "acts and words in such a form that those who read them may judge for themselves of the merits and defects of the policy he has pursued." Although advertised as an "IMPARTIAL, TRUTHFUL, AND STANDARD" account of Lincoln's administration by the publisher Derby and Miller, it was, considering its author, anything but impartial. Produced by the man running the National Union Party's campaign, this work should be considered a party publication.[7]

After Lincoln was renominated, Raymond expanded the biographical account that appeared in his history of the administration for a smaller and less expensive publication, *The Life of Abraham Lincoln*, issued in paper wrappers, with a wood engraving of Lincoln on the cover. Published in separate editions by Derby and Miller and the National Union Executive Committee, the book consists of 136 pages, including John Savage's 50-page biography of Andrew Johnson, the National Union Party's vice presidential candidate. Raymond's expanded biographical account was more affordable than his massive earlier work, which was published in cloth at a price of $1.50.[8]

Cover of Henry J. Raymond's *The Life of Abraham Lincoln* (New York: National Union Executive Committee, 1864). The book includes a biography of the National Union Party's vice presidential candidate, Andrew Johnson, by John Savage. Courtesy of the John Hay Library, Brown University.

Joseph H. Barrett, author of another 1860 Lincoln campaign biography, produced a work that included, with "slight modifications," his earlier account of Lincoln's life along with a history of his presidency up through the first months of 1864. Published in Cincinnati either before the National Union Party convention or within a day or two after its closing, Barrett's five-hundred-page book, which includes a Buttre steel engraving of the president based on a Brady photograph, was issued in cloth at a cost (at least one dollar) that may have limited its accessibility to the average voter.[9]

The Philadelphia publishing house of T. B. Peterson and Brothers issued a Lincoln campaign biography before the National Union Party assembled in Baltimore. Written by David Brainerd Williamson (1827–1900) and issued in both paper and cloth editions, *The Life and Public Services of Abraham Lincoln* includes a wood engraving of the president on the cover of the paper version.[10] Another campaign biography that was published before Lincoln's renomination was written by Orville James Victor (1827–1910), the longtime editor and writer for Beadle and Company's various publishing ventures. *Private and Public Life of Abraham Lincoln*, which covers the candidate's life through 1863 and issued as number fourteen of Beadle and Company's Dime Biographical Library, was published as a small paperback that could be fit into a reader's pocket. The cover of the volume depicts Lincoln as a boy honing his reading skills by the light of the hearth fire, a homespun image that conveys the message that pervades the Beadle series, that one can achieve success through determination, hard work, and perseverance. Although the intended purpose of Victor's biography was to present Lincoln's life, including his presidency, as a moral lesson, it also served another purpose—promoting the president's reelection. One historian asserts that this little booklet was "popular among soldiers," some of whom were avid readers of several Beadle series.[11]

Campaign biographies of Lincoln that were published after his renomination include *The Life of Abraham Lincoln* by pseudonymous author Abbot A. Abbott, a thirty-page pamphlet issued by the Union League of Philadelphia, an anonymously written pamphlet entitled *A Workingman's Reasons for the Re-Election of Abraham Lincoln*, and

Cover of Orville J. Victor's *Private and Public Life of Abraham Lincoln* (New York: Beadle & Co., 1860) that depicts young Lincoln reading by the light of the family hearth. Courtesy of the John Hay Library, Brown University.

a chapter in J. M. Hiatt's book on the political history of the United States, which includes brief sketches of the candidates for president, including John C. Frémont.[12] Finally, there was *Character and Public Services of Abraham Lincoln* by the newspaper editor and author of juvenile books, William Makepeace Thayer (1820–98). It was published in Boston in several versions by two different publishers in both paper and cloth editions. The paper edition was issued as "The 'Campaign Document,'" and includes a crude wood engraving of the president as well as steel-engraved frontispieces of Lincoln and the log cabin in which he was born. Thayer's *The Pioneer Boy*, a popular boys' book on Lincoln's rise to the presidency, was published in 1863.[13]

The image of Lincoln that his party and his biographers shaped and promoted in 1864 was of a president who faced the most serious crisis in the nation's history and through coolness, courage, confidence, resolve, foresight, and competent leadership had held the rebellion in check, prevented the complete destruction of the Union, and emancipated the enslaved. For most of Lincoln's biographers, the image of the honest, rail-splitting man of the people was still relevant, as it was used to explain Lincoln's success as president.

Many biographers contend that Lincoln's character was as central to his success as president as it was in his life before 1860. In their view, one could not appreciate Lincoln's strength of character without understanding his humble upbringing and the many struggles he faced as a young man. "Surely the successes of his early life were harbingers of triumphs in this period of sanguinary strife," declares Thayer. "The elements of character that adorned his youth, and blossomed into golden manhood," he asserts, "prefigured his successful administration of national affairs as the ruler of the American Republic."[14] Victor expands on this theme, resurrecting the image of Lincoln overcoming the primitive log cabin experience of his youth through hard work and disciplined self-education.

> By the dim light of the pioneer's hearth—by the candle in the log loft—by the lamp in the musty office, he wrought out his task. While others slept, he found repose in the realms of knowledge. While he labored, with zeal, at the ax, at the plow,

Cover of William M. Thayer's *Character and Public Services of Abraham Lincoln* (Boston: Dinsmoor & Co., 1864). Courtesy of the John Hay Library, Brown University.

Cover of the anonymously written *The Life of Abraham Lincoln* (New York: T. R. Dawley, 1864), depicting vignettes from Lincoln's life, including the log cabin in which he was born and images of him splitting rails and steering a flatboat. Courtesy of the John Hay Library, Brown University.

at the harvest, at the sweeps of the flatboat, his eager soul was laying away its treasures won from books, from experience, from men—from every thing which could impart information. The years of hardest experience, therefore, were years of development and mental progress; and it would seem, when viewed by the light of succeeding events, that that early experience was a school of Providence to fit him for the mighty struggle which he was to direct.[15]

Lincoln's character, molded by the rugged frontier environment, prepared him for the extraordinary challenges of his presidency. As one biographer notes, no president "ever encountered the same difficulties which have met the present incumbent of the 'White House' at every step he has taken since the day of his inauguration."[16] Raymond and the other biographers agreed: the crisis faced by Lincoln was unprecedented. "No one of his predecessors, not even Washington," Raymond argues, "encountered difficulties of equal magnitude, or was called to perform duties of equal magnitude." Elected by a minority of the popular vote, with his election blamed by some as the cause of the Civil War, Lincoln was called upon to address the momentous crisis, a task that proved to be "one of the most gigantic that ever fell to the lot of the head of any nation."[17] Another biographer claims that no man other than Lincoln "ever entered office in our history whose duties were so difficult, whose responsibilities were so great, or whose path was so beset by danger and embarrassment. War had suddenly broke [sic] out in the country which so long had lapped in the blessings of peace, plenty, and security, that it was wholly unprepared for war."[18]

Lincoln's success in managing the long and bloody war and his achievements, especially the emancipation of slaves, are attributed to several character traits he brought to the presidency. Many biographers point to the president's honesty and integrity as integral to securing the trust of the people of the North. According to Barrett, Lincoln's policy "has been fully set forth in his own words. No dissembling, no insincerity, gives the least false tinge to any of his public papers or addresses. This outspoken, frank, confiding way of his, has given him hold upon the popular heart, and upon the love of all true men, such as few statesmen have ever had."[19]

"By universal acclaim he is '*honest old Abe*,'" writes another Lincoln biographer. And in the midst of trials and tribulations of the Civil War, "there was one man whom the people felt would never betray them, and that man was their own President."[20] This sentiment is echoed by Raymond, who contends that no man whose honesty "was open to suspicion, no matter what might have been his abilities or his experience, could possibly have retained enough of public confidence to carry the country through such a contest as that in which we are now involved." Because no one suspected Lincoln of seeking his own aggrandizement or abusing the powers of his office at the expense of his country's liberties, the people of the North "lavishly and eagerly conferred upon him" their trust and loyalty.[21] Thayer gives thanks to "a good Providence" for sending the people "a ruler whose honesty is 'clear as the sun, fair as the moon,' and, to our malignant foes, 'terrible as an army with banners'!"[22]

Another theme of the biographers is that "The People" trust and support Lincoln because he is perceived as one of them. He speaks the language of the "common people," insists Raymond: "he has no pride of intellect—not the slightest desire for display—no thought or purpose but that of making everybody understand precisely what he believes and means to utter." Thayer, too, waxes admiringly about Lincoln's connection to ordinary people. "He appears to regard his fellow-men as equals," and acts upon the principle "that neither office nor honor can add true worth to manhood." Despite holding the highest office in the land, Lincoln "is as familiar, genial, and loving as he ever was; and . . . possesses that remarkable faculty of making everybody feel at home in his presence."[23]

Lincoln was more than a friend to ordinary Americans; he also served as a father figure, especially to young soldiers who donned a uniform to fight bravely for the Union cause. Lincoln's admiration, respect, and sympathy for soldiers, explains Thayer, is why the president "is endeared to our loyal army," and a bond of "mutual love and respect is cherished between them." There are "many instances of his unfeigned attachment to the soldier," including countless "errands of sympathy and love to the wards of the hospitals."[24] The issue of Lincoln's close relationship with the common soldier, many of whom referred to him as "Father Abraham," rose in importance after the Democrats nominated General McClellan, known for securing the love and loyalty of his troops.[25]

Other character traits highlighted by Lincoln's campaign biographers are coolness in the face of setbacks, resolve under fire from both Radical Republicans and Democratic Copperheads, a superior intellect, and, according to one writer, being a "student of Providence." A key to Lincoln's success, in the opinion of Thayer, is his willingness to acknowledge "the hand of God in events." Moreover, he is a man without moral stain, since his habits "are as simple and pure to-day as they were in his early manhood." A man who "never smokes, never uses intoxicating drinks, never utters a profane word, or engages in games of chance . . . is unusual in the political world." The president's moral and pious habits protect him "against the seductions of office or honor."[26]

Several campaign biographies move beyond merely describing Lincoln's virtues to linking them directly to his actions as president. A strong character formed on the Western frontier, molded by a strict regimen of self-education, prepared Lincoln to assume the mantle of leadership and the role of father of his country originally defined by George Washington. Lincoln's management of the war, his Emancipation Proclamation, his suspension of habeas corpus, and his institution of a draft are vigorously defended by his campaign biographers. The Emancipation Proclamation is hailed by Barrett as "inaugurating a new era in the progress of the war" and "a landmark in the nation's history for all time." The proclamation restored the faith and revived the confidence of those who "now saw the only hope of a complete overthrow of the slaveholders' conspiracy, in the utter eradication of its mischievous and immoral cause." Moreover, in Europe, "the line was now distinctly drawn between the grand principles of universal freedom and the usurpations of slaveholding barbarism; between legitimate authority on the side of liberty, and [that] organized to perpetuate oppression."[27] Raymond contends that although Lincoln's proclamation "has not accomplished all that some expected it to do," it "drew to our side more unmistakably the sympathies of the friends of freedom everywhere, and shut up the path of the friends of rebellion." In addition, it brought "thousands" of courageous blacks into the Union Army.[28] Another biographer considers the preliminary and final versions of the proclamation the "two most important proclamations ever penned by a President of the United States."[29]

Despite their hearty support of Lincoln's policy concerning emancipation and his use of the war powers of his office against Confederate sympathizers in the North, two biographers go out of their way to assure readers that the president was no radical. Raymond claims that Lincoln consistently stood up to Radical Republicans as well as Democratic Copperheads while pursuing a moderate course. "His policy has been from the outset a tentative one," avers Raymond, as all policies of government "to be successful must always be." Thayer echoes this sentiment, declaring that Lincoln, with "two violent factions on almost every question pressing their respective claims," has "pursued an even-handed course . . . that has disarmed their animosity and resulted in greater harmony."[30]

Campaign biographers are quick to point out that Lincoln's politically astute, prudent course on issues such as emancipation, habeas corpus, confiscation of Confederate property, and the draft were supported by a large majority of Northerners. "The power exercised by President Lincoln in suspending the writ of habeas corpus," states Barrett, "gave some uneasiness to a class of men whose efforts to obstruct the Government in putting down the rebellion had been pursued under the assumption that they would escape punishment . . . for the treason for which they were morally guilty," but the measure was "fully sustained" by the people. While suspension of the writ of habeas corpus, emancipation, the confiscation acts, and the draft may have been violently criticized by enemies of the government, they were, claims Thayer, supported by loyal Northerners, who are "never so united as now."[31]

One writer goes so far as to credit Lincoln's 1860 election and success as president to divine intervention. "If he has risen so far above his companions in early toil, it is because God had endowed him with that rare superiority of intellect which no combination of disadvantages can depress or obscure," explains an anonymous author of a campaign tract. "And now, in this great man, sprung from the ranks of the people, ought we not to see and acknowledge the hand of a special Providence . . . may not a retributive hand of a just God be recognized" in the elevation of such a man "to avenge the wrongs of the people, and to put down a rebellion that seeks the establishment of monarchy and privileged orders upon the ruin of their equal rights?"[32]

Not surprisingly, all of Lincoln's campaign biographers proclaim the president's first term a success, regardless of whether it was guided by divine providence, the result of Lincoln's leadership abilities, or a combination of both. All stress, however, that Lincoln's work is not complete: the war must be won, the United States must endure. The nation's future depends on the reelection of Abraham Lincoln. For example, the author of *A Workingman's Reasons for the Re-Election of Abraham Lincoln* urges readers to give the president the chance to complete the work commenced in his first term. "Justice demands" a fair trial for his policies, "and that cannot be had without his reelection for a second term." After all, the writer argues, Lincoln's reelection would secure the restoration of the Union by rendering "the most fatal of blows . . . to the hopes of the rebels."[33]

The Union League of Philadelphia urged citizens of Pennsylvania to return Lincoln as commander in chief because the stake in the war "is no less than our country." Under such perilous circumstances, "it behooves us to place great power in competent hands. Integrity, courage, talents, knowledge are necessary to save the country in its hour of trial and danger. And because it is such a critical time in the nation's history, the Executive Department is especially called upon for prompt, determined, wise, and prudent action," which Americans had come to expect from Lincoln.[34]

Thayer warns against changing presidents in time of war. After all, "to change our President in the face of the enemy would be as suicidal as to change a competent general on the eve of battle." Lincoln deserves reelection because he has grappled with the greatest crisis in American history and yet has maintained, under "firm and resolute guidance," a government that "stands forth to-day as a model of national forbearance, to challenge the admiration of the world." And he is qualified "to do even better" during a second term because "he has now that best of all qualifications—Experience. He has become acquainted with the machine, and knows how to run it."[35] Lincoln, contends Williamson, "has proved himself equal to *the emergency*" facing the nation. He "has been tried, and not found wanting, and no better return for the perils encountered, the labors accomplished, and the benefits derived to the country" than his reelection. After all, Lincoln "is no longer the representative of any particular political party, but comes before the loyal voters as an indefatigable, incorruptible, public servant" who has "never failed to prove himself equal to any emergency that might occur." Williamson's case for Lincoln's reelection is that he, like Washington before him, has passed the test of leadership, has put partisan politics aside, to become a father figure to a nation that is, once again, fighting for its future.[36]

This positive image of Lincoln—man of the people who had become a trusted father–figure to Americans loyal to the Union—conveyed through campaign biographies and other genres of print was fashioned to counter an opposing image designed by his critics of a despot willing to wage a bloody, destructive war while shredding the Constitution in order to end slavery, establish equal rights for blacks, and subjugate the Southern people. As discussed in a previous chapter, Lincoln's opponents in 1860 tread carefully when criticizing him, questioning his qualifications for the presidency without denigrating the image of the rail-splitting, self-made Westerner that many Americans could relate to and admire. In 1860, Lincoln was portrayed more as an unwitting pawn of a radical Republican Party willing to divide the country and bring on a civil war by forcing its abolitionist ideology on the South. As we have seen, Lincoln in 1860, despite his compelling life story, tended to be depicted by opponents as an uneducated, uncouth country lawyer who was unqualified for the nation's highest office. Whatever criticism Lincoln faced in 1860, however, was tame compared to what he endured during his presidency and, especially, the 1864 election season.

During his first term, Lincoln was often criticized by Radical Republicans as being too slow both in ending slavery and pursuing a harsh war on the South, and regularly condemned by conservative Democrats as too radical concerning slavery and overly aggressive in the use of the war powers against critics of his administration. The most hostile and racially charged assaults on Lincoln's character and presidency came from Peace Democrats, or Copperheads, in the wake of his suspension of habeas corpus, the Emancipation Proclamation, and other administration measures criticized as unconstitutional abuses of executive power.

Two 1864 Copperhead-inspired publications exemplify the virulent racist attacks on Lincoln. Alexander Delmar or Del Mar (1836–1926), a political economist, historian, and writer who supported the Democratic Party and wrote a campaign biography of George McClellan, also wrote a pamphlet entitled *Abraham Africanus I*. In it, Delmar uses biting sarcasm to indict Lincoln as an infidel who made a pact with the devil in order to become king of the United States. The cover includes an image of Lincoln wearing a royal crown. J. F. Feeks, the New York firm that issued *Abraham Africanus I*, also published *The Lincoln Catechism*, replete with an image of a smiling black man on the cover. Serving as a companion piece to *Abraham Africanus I*, this publication poses a series of questions and provides answers that lampoon Lincoln as a dictator named Abraham Africanus intent on forcing on the American people emancipation, miscegenation, and other despotic atrocities. Although these works address more than Lincoln's—and by extension, the Republican Party's—policies concerning slavery and black Americans, they unapologetically use racist language and images when ridiculing the president. Examples of several questions and answers included in the *Lincoln Catechism* set the tone of what one encounters throughout the pamphlet: "By whom hath the Constitution been made obsolete? By Abraham Africanus the First. To what end? That his days may be long in office—and that he may make himself and his people the equal of the negroes. What is a President? A general agent for negroes."[37]

Attacks such as these, playing on white Americans' fears of racial equality and miscegenation, took a toll on Lincoln's standing

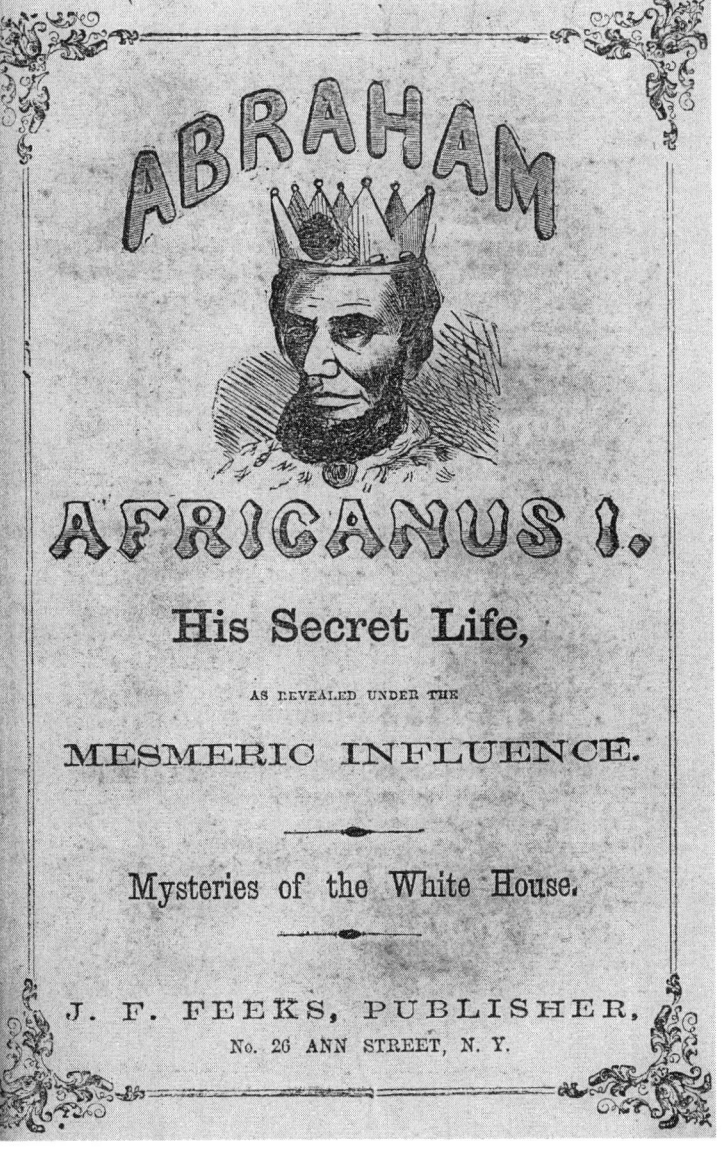

Cover of *Abraham Africanus I* (New York: J. F. Feeks, 1864). Courtesy of the John Hay Library, Brown University.

with the Northern public, especially as casualties and defeats on the battlefield continued to mount. But while the increasing effectiveness of the Copperhead's anti-Lincoln campaign may have weakened the president's prospects for reelection, their strong antiwar stance caused significant problems for the Democratic Party's nominee. The Democrats' convention was scheduled to open in Chicago on July 4, weeks after the Republican gathering in Baltimore. But Peace Democrats were able to convince party leaders to postpone the convention until August 29, believing that by a later date the military situation, and thus Lincoln's support, would have eroded to such a point that they would be in a stronger position to dictate a peace platform and nominate a peace candidate. With their leader Clement Vallandigham chairing the platform committee, Copperheads got the platform they wanted, with a plank labeling the war a failure and calling for a convention to produce a treaty that would end the war and restore the "Federal Union of the States." Despite Copperhead efforts to nominate a candidate of their choice, convention delegates ended up picking General George B. McClellan, who was popular with many War Democrats. The general rejected the party's peace plank, vowing to make reunion a precondition for any peace treaty. Yet, following the advice of War Democrats who feared alienating the Copperhead faction, McClellan announced that he would not make emancipation a pre-condition for peace. He could not have been happy with the party's nominee for vice president, a hard-line peace Democrat from Ohio, George Pendleton.[38]

The Democratic Party's platform became a millstone around McClellan's neck as a result of a dramatic turn of events on the war front. On September 1, the day after his nomination in Chicago, Atlanta fell to General William Tecumseh Sherman's Union forces. This victory, in conjunction with Admiral David Farragut's victory at Mobile Bay and General Philip Sheridan's successful campaign in the Shenandoah Valley, called into question the Democrats' platform plank on the war and damaged severely McClellan's hopes for the presidency.

Like Lincoln, McClellan did not campaign personally. Campaign managers and party operatives organized speeches, rallies, and parades and, along with commercial publishing firms, oversaw the dissemination of pro-McClellan publications, including campaign biographies, and anti-Lincoln materials.[39] Two biographies were published by party organizations and eight by commercial firms. Many of these works contain wood or steel engravings of the general.[40] There was also a burlesque biography published, which, like those issued about Lincoln, appeared to be neither for nor against the candidate.

A major challenge facing the McClellan campaign pertained to its message: proposing an alternate course on the war without being cast as pro-Confederate sympathizers or traitors as Republicans and War Democrats were quick to label McClellan and his supporters. Thus the image of McClellan promoted by his campaign biographies is of a devoted patriot, a genuine war hero, and a man of strong character who would end the war with honor, reunite the country, respect the Constitution, protect individual liberties, and reject fanatical attempts to rearrange the social order by forcing equal rights for blacks. He is presented as a dedicated public servant mistreated by an incompetent, uncivilized, militarily ignorant president and his radical advisers. According to his biographers, McClellan, unlike Lincoln, was raised by cultured, socially prominent parents to become a gentleman and a scholar who graduated second in his class from West Point. Having served with gallantry in the Mexican War, McClellan was one of the first to answer Lincoln's call for volunteers in the wake of the attack on Fort Sumter. Having led his troops in the Union Army's first victories in the war, he was appointed by the president to lead the Army of the Potomac, which he organized into one of the greatest fighting forces in history.

All of his biographers emphasize the relentless and unfair criticism directed at their subject, despite his success in organizing the Army of the Potomac, leading it to the outskirts of the Confederate capital of Richmond, and his victory at Antietam. They argue that he could have captured the Confederate capital if he had received adequate reinforcements from the president. Yet all he received from Lincoln, his advisers, and radical Republicans was blame for moving too slowly or not moving at all. One biographer, George S. Hillard, defends McClellan by comparing the general to military heroes of the past, Washington and Lord Wellington, who also were "constantly censured for their slowness." McClellan, Hillard admits, "is, by nature and temperament, wisely cautious, prudent, and deliberate. . . . He never incurs great risks or plays a desperate game" because he is "a humane man, very careful of the lives of his soldiers, and not needlessly shedding human blood." As a wise and experienced military man, McClellan would never "be induced by popular clamor to take a step which he deems unwise, or forgo a precaution which he deems necessary." In a knock on the president and his military advises, Hillard asserts that only those "who are least qualified to form a correct judgment" would ask a general to risk his strategic advantage and his men by taking rash actions.[41]

Even though McClellan compiled a brilliant military record, never losing a battle; saved Washington from attack by defeating General Lee's army at Antietam; and was loved by his soldiers, in November of 1862 he was unjustly removed from command of the Army of the Potomac by an ungrateful president and his "fanatical Administration."[42] As a result of this disgraceful move, bemoans one biographer, the Army of the Potomac is still in the "very spot where McClellan left it seventeen months ago." Furthermore, "it has lost fifty thousand men, and is not an inch nearer Richmond." "The people of the North," the writer continues," each night and morning, send up to Heaven a fervent prayer to be rid of the wretched fanatics who have destroyed the Union, violated the Constitution, and are now leaving no effort unemployed to overthrow republicanism, and set up a despotism."[43]

Alexander Delmar argues that McClellan was relieved of his command because he "was in the way" of Lincoln and his radical advisers. He was seen as an obstacle to the administration's nefarious, shifting agenda, from waging a war to save the Union to one of "subjugation," of the free and emancipation of the enslaved, which mandated a harsh war against Southern civilians and the confiscation of their property.[44] Crushing the rebellion is a rightful purpose of the war, affirms James Gallatin, but in doing so it is "not requisite to *exterminate* the *people* of the South." "Arbitrary imprisonment and punishment" of Northern critics of the administration's policies, "odious instruments of despotic power," would cease under a McClellan presidency. His administration will conduct a civilized war against rebel armies, not a destructive one against Southern civilians. Moreover, he will not "destroy the Constitution to complete the destruction of any national evil;" he will "destroy every such evil in accordance with the principles of the Constitution." In other words, he will not "set the house on fire, and burn it down, in order to clean out the soot that had gathered in the chimney." He will "clean out the chimney."[45]

There is scant mention of McClellan's private or domestic life in his campaign biographies. Not surprisingly, readers learn that the Democratic candidate is a moral man with many noble traits. McClellan is praised by Gallatin as "direct, energetic, and decisive," possessing a "straightforward honesty." His character is a "reflex of that of Washington in his religious devotion;" the same "spotless purity of private life, which distinguished the one, characterizes the other."[46] "The character of McClellan, according to another biographer, "has won the highest admiration not only of the patriotic in America, but of every anxious spectator of the American war in foreign lands." As a general, he "secured the love of his soldiers" and the "fear of his enemy. He was humane and tolerant, and waged war only against armed men, never against the unarmed and defenseless. He made no raids to destroy private property; burned no towns; employed no mercenaries; incited no slaves to revolt." Like Washington before him, McClellan "is the first in the hearts of the people, for that high office—once, and we trust again to be, the reward of virtue—which, as he has neither sought it, the nation trusts he will not decline it."[47]

Abraham Lincoln was re-elected by a wide electoral margin over his Democratic opponent, carrying twenty-two states (212 electoral votes) to McClellan's three (21 electoral votes) and winning more than 55 percent of the popular vote. Included in Lincoln's popular tally was an overwhelming soldier vote, which must have been a severe disappointment to McClellan. The soldier vote, estimated at 4 percent of the total popular vote, went for Father Abraham by 78 percent to 22 percent for McClellan.[48] It was a remarkable victory for the president considering the long and bloody war he led, the many setbacks the Union Army endured, and the controversial measures his administration initiated. Would Lincoln have prevailed if Sherman had not taken Atlanta when he did or if Farragut and Sheridan had not been successful in their campaigns in Mobile Bay or in the Shenandoah Valley? Would Northern voters, frustrated and tired of a war going badly, have turned their backs on the rail splitter who had become to many a trusted father figure? We will never know.

CONCLUSION:
BIOGRAPHIES AND BALLOTS

The "Honest Abe, the Rail Splitter" image of Lincoln that emerged from the Illinois and national Republican conventions in the spring of 1860 was appealing to many Northern voters and especially to those voters residing in Western states. Republican leaders like Lincoln who participated in or remembered the Whig "Log Cabin" campaign of 1840—or even the Zachary Taylor "Rough and Ready" campaign of 1848—were acutely aware of the power of imagery and symbolism. If a log cabin and hard cider elected William Henry Harrison then, a log cabin and an axe could elect Abraham Lincoln in 1860. The homespun representation of Lincoln as a rugged, honest, self-made, common man from the West who triumphed over the many challenges encountered in frontier life through hard work, moral as well as physical strength, and an innate rather than a school-learned intelligence, was one to which many Americans, especially those living in similar circumstances, could relate.

This image of Lincoln merged with the Republican Party's platform supporting a free-labor, free-soil ideology that opposed the extension of slavery and advocated government-sponsored economic development. This ideology was promoted by the party at speeches, parades, rallies, and, with the assistance of commercial publishing houses, disseminated though a diverse array of printed matter, such as newspapers, broadsides, prints, songsters, sheet music, and, of course campaign biographies. While many potential voters were introduced to the Lincoln image through various forms of print, they may not have understood completely the larger context of its meaning. Whereas many genres of print provided voters with a snapshot of a candidate's career and virtues, campaign biographies offered in one place the most extensive amount of information concerning a candidate's life, character, and qualifications for office.

The Republican Party's nomination in 1860 of a rustic, axe-wielding, self-made Western man of the people captured the attention of the publishing industry and commercial firms. Several publishers, sensing the rags-to-almost-riches story of Lincoln's life would be profoundly appealing to consumers, issued campaign biographies of the candidate within weeks of his nomination. It appears that, judging by the appearance of multiple editions and variants, a few of these biographies sold well. That several of these publications regularly appear in today's market indicates that at least two or three had large print runs, indicating the publisher's assumption that they would sell. While the cloth editions of Lincoln's campaign biographies, averaging one dollar in price, were beyond the financial reach of many Americans, biographies issued in paper wrappers, ranging in price from twenty-five to fifty cents, were affordable to many.

When Lincoln ran for reelection in 1864 he was no longer an unknown Western lawyer. He was president of the United States with a record to defend. After three years of a bloody civil war and in the wake of controversial measures concerning habeas corpus, emancipation of the enslaved, confiscation of Confederate property, and institution of a draft, Lincoln required no introduction. He was well known to Northern voters, revered by some and reviled by others. Meanwhile, the "Honest Abe, the Rail-Splitter" image, while inadequate by itself for the 1864 election, retained its appeal and, more important, its relevance, at least to those writing campaign biographies. The image of 1860 was resurrected by biographers to remind voters of the qualities that initially endeared them to Lincoln and how these virtues informed his actions as president. The man who had become the beloved and trusted father figure to loyal Northerners, especially to the brave soldiers who defended the

Union, brought to the presidency a strong, moral character, marked by courage, confidence, integrity, and resolve that was shaped by the Western frontier. He was loved by the people because he was one of them; he was trusted by them because they believed in "Honest Abe." The "Rail Splitter" had become "Father Abraham." This was the image conveyed through the 1864 Lincoln campaign biographies as well as through other forms of print issued during that election season.

Lincoln's campaign biographies, for the most part, conform to the formula established by writers of previous works of this nature. (The same can also be said of those written on behalf of Douglas, Bell, Breckinridge, and McClellan.) Readers of these works encountered virtues in Lincoln associated with candidates of previous presidential elections. Lincoln's life story, like that of all virtuous and moral men, was inspiring and worth emulating. There was a slight divergence from the norm in Lincoln's 1864 biographies, however. In these works, Lincoln's biography is used primarily as a backdrop to a spirited defense of his presidency. By 1864, presidential campaign biographies of incumbents were rare. Since the emergence of the genre in 1824, only three presidential elections (1828, 1832, and 1840) featured incumbents running for reelection. From 1824 to 1860 seven elections involved candidates running for the first time who warranted varying degrees of introduction to American voters.

The positive images of Lincoln promoted by his supporters and disseminated through print were challenged by competing images in both elections. Not only were there campaign biographies of his opponents, but there were scores of anti-Lincoln images and symbols accessible to voters. By the 1864 election, attacks on Lincoln and his administration had become as vitriolic as they had become commonplace. What effect did these competing images and messages have on Americans' perceptions of Lincoln? What role did Lincoln's campaign biographies play in his election and reelection? One can safely assume that Lincoln's campaign biographies resonated with some voters and convinced some to vote for him in 1860 and 1864. But did they energize and convince enough voters to make a difference in the outcomes of these elections?

Answering these questions requires documentation and evidence that are, unfortunately, frustratingly elusive to the historian. Sales figures for Lincoln's campaign biographies—as well as those of his opponents—are virtually nonexistent. We do not know how many of these works were printed, let alone sold. But even if reliable statistics on print runs and sales were available, they would not provide the evidence that gets to the heart of the questions posed above. How many people read the biographies? Of those that did read one or more campaign biographies, what did they take away from the reading experience? And what actions or reactions did these publications inspire? It is difficult, if not impossible, to adduce how people read and what attitudes they brought to or took away from a reading experience even when other forms of documentation exist. What evidence does exist is anecdotal and fragmented. In this instance, all one can do is infer or speculate based on the meager evidence at hand.

In terms of the 1860 election, there were sixteen Lincoln campaign biographies, compared to eighteen for his three opponents combined. There are indications that several of Lincoln's biographies sold well. Moreover, the image of Lincoln promoted by his biographies—as well as through other genres of print—appeared to connect with ordinary Americans. Judging by the various symbols that adorned broadsides, posters, sheet music, banners, and other campaign materials, the Rail-Splitter image was popular with the Republican Party faithful and embraced by the commercial sector. And that image, along with that of Lincoln as the Great Emancipator, has endured, found on the covers of and illustrations in numerous books, especially those geared to children and young adults, and in scores of prints and engravings, movies, and various works of art.[1]

To reiterate what was mentioned above, some voters would have been introduced to Lincoln and his life story through reading a campaign biography; others would have voted for Lincoln based on some other biographical account they read or even heard. But did campaign biographies make a difference in the 1860 campaign, or in the 1864 contest, for that matter? In all likelihood, they did not hurt and probably helped Lincoln's chances. But Lincoln's inspiring biography—and the images associated with it—was one of several elements that worked in the candidate's favor. Critical factors in the 1860 election were the split among Democrats and the presence of a third-party candidate; the growing popularity in the North and West of the Republican message of free labor and free soil, prohibiting slavery in the territories, federal support for internal improvements; and the issue of corruption in the Buchanan administration. In addition, voters who showed up at the polls to vote for Lincoln may have been motivated by other factors, such as party loyalty, local issues, religious concerns, or ethnic solidarity.[2]

One wonders, however, what the outcome of the 1860 election would have been if Douglas or another compromise Democratic candidate had been Lincoln's sole opponent, or if there were no Constitutional Union Party to nominate John Bell.[3] And in 1864, would Lincoln have been reelected if Sherman had not captured Atlanta when he did? Would the "Father Abraham" image evoked by his campaign biographers have convinced enough voters to stick with the man they voted for in 1860? Prior to Atlanta's fall, Henry Raymond, chair of the National Union Party and one of Lincoln's biographers, as well as Lincoln himself, believed the election was as good as lost.

The inability to answer several key questions concerning the impact of Lincoln's campaign biographies does not lessen the value of these publications in terms of what can be learned from them. This underappreciated and unstudied genre provides a lens through which scholars can examine what party leaders, commercial firms, the American reading public, and, in some cases, candidates thought were the essential qualities of character and leadership in a particular time in our history, and how they used the printed word to disseminate images and symbols that, in modern-day parlance, packaged and promoted these attributes. In 1860 and 1864, an American voter seeking information regarding Lincoln the candidate or a refresher course on Lincoln the president, had several forms of print at their disposal. Of these, the campaign biography was the only source that provided in one place the most extensive amount of information concerning his life. It would be foolish, of course, to claim that Lincoln's campaign biographies were the deciding factors in his electoral victories. One can argue, however, that at the very least, these works both reinforced and shaped readers' positive assumptions and views concerning Lincoln, introduced him to new voters, and perhaps changed the minds of those who were unsure or wary of the man who was touted as "Honest Abe, the Rail Splitter" or as "Father Abraham."

ACKNOWLEDGMENTS
NOTES
SELECTED BIBLIOGRAPHY
INDEX

ACKNOWLEDGMENTS

I thank Southern Illinois University Press for the opportunity to participate in the Concise Lincoln Library series. I am grateful for the comments, criticisms, and suggestions offered by series editors Richard W. Etulain, Sara Vaughn Gabbard, and Sylvia Frank Rodrigue, as well as those from the anonymous outside reader. This is my second book working with Sylvia Frank Rodrigue. I can't think of a more caring, kind, and competent editor to work with than Sylvia. It has been a real pleasure. Thanks also to Wayne Larsen, project editor, and Barb Martin, manager of editing, design, and production at SIU Press. They helped to make this a better book. As for any errors found in it, I take full responsibility.

I also thank Jonathan H. Mann of the Rail Splitter, an organization of Lincoln collectors, for his support and for permission to use one of the illustrations in this book. The John Hay Library at Brown University kindly permitted me to use all of the remaining illustrations that appear herein. I especially thank Holly Snyder, curator of American History at the Hay Library, for all her help in gathering the illustrations.

Finally, I thank my wife, Beth, whose loving support for my research and writing keeps me going and whose patience allows me to spend far too much time with Abraham Lincoln. This book is dedicated to her.

NOTES

Introduction

1. This account of the 1860 Illinois Republican convention is based on the following works: Michael S. Green, *Lincoln and the Election of 1860* (Carbondale and Edwardsville: Southern Illinois University Press, 2011), 47–50; Michael Burlingame, *Abraham Lincoln: A Life*, 2 vols. (Baltimore: Johns Hopkins University Press, 2008), 1: 597–600; William C. Harris, *Lincoln's Rise to the Presidency* (Lawrence: University Press of Kansas, 2007), 197; David Herbert Donald, *Lincoln* (New York: Simon and Schuster, 1995), 244–46; and Wayne C. Temple, "Lincoln's Fence Rails," *Journal of the Illinois State Historical Society* 47 (Spring 1954): 20–34.
2. Burlingame, *Abraham Lincoln*, 1: 599; Temple, "Lincoln's Fence Rails," 21–23.
3. *Illinois State Journal*, May 11, 1860, quoted in Temple, "Lincoln's Fence Rails," 26.
4. "Remarks to Republican State Convention, Decatur, Illinois," May 9, 1860, in Abraham Lincoln, *Collected Works of Abraham Lincoln,* 9 vols., ed. Roy P. Basler (New Brunswick, N.J.: Rutgers University Press), 4: 48. (Hereafter cited as *CW*). The day before the convention opened, the *Illinois State Journal* had informed readers that rails split and mauled by Lincoln would be on view. One finds it hard to believe Lincoln's claim that he knew nothing about the rails being introduced at the convention, since he was an avid reader of newspapers and would have followed any news about the upcoming convention, especially if it pertained to him.
5. The journalist Noah Brooks claimed that Lincoln "was not greatly pleased with the rail incident." Quoted in Burlingame, *Abraham Lincoln*, 1: 598.
6. Ibid., 1: 599–600.
7. Green, *Lincoln and the Election of 1860*, 51–62. See also Gary Ecelbarger, *The Great Comeback: How Abraham Lincoln Beat the Odds to Win the 1860 Republican Nomination* (New York: St. Martin's Press, 2008).
8. On the symbolic image of the split-rail fence, see Adam Goodheart, *1861: The Civil War Awakening* (New York: Alfred A. Knopf, 2011), 35. On free-labor ideology in antebellum America, see Eric Foner, *Free Soil, Free Labor, Free Men: The Ideology of the Republican Party before the Civil War* (New York: Oxford University Press, 1970). See also Gabor S. Boritt, *Lincoln and the Economics of the American Dream* (Memphis: Memphis State University Press, 1978); and Thomas E. Rodgers, "Saving

the Republic: Turnout, Ideology, and Republicanism in the Election of 1860," in *The Election of 1860 Reconsidered*, ed. A. James Fuller (Kent, Ohio: Kent State University Press, 2013), 165–92.
9. On the charges of corruption against the Buchanan administration and congressional investigations concerning these charges, see Jean H. Baker, *James Buchanan* (New York: Henry Holt, 2004), 113–16; and Thomas A. Horrocks, *President James Buchanan and the Crisis of National Leadership* (New York: Nova Science Publishers, 2012), 78–81. See also John W. Quist and Michael J. Birkner, eds., *James Buchanan and the Coming of the Civil War* (Gainesville: University Press of Florida, 2013).
10. Green, *Lincoln and the Election of 1860*. See also Douglas Egerton, *Year of Meteors: Stephen Douglas, Abraham Lincoln, and the Election That Brought on the Civil War* (New York: Bloomsbury Press, 2010); and Fuller, *The Election of 1860 Reconsidered*.

1. Texts, Contexts, and Contests: Politics and Print in the Age of Lincoln

1. *Chicago Press and Tribune*, May 15, 1860, cited in *Abraham Lincoln: A Press Portrait*, ed. Herbert Mitgang (Athens: University of Georgia Press, 1989), 164–65. One suspects that the reference to Lincoln's "unexceptional" record meant that it was not as controversial as that of the presumed favorite, Senator William H. Seward of New York.
2. Letter to Lyman Trumbull, April 29, 1860, in *CW*, 4: 45.
3. Joel H. Silbey, *The American Political Nation, 1838–1893* (Stanford: Stanford University Press, 1991), 10–26. Thomas Jefferson to Francis Hopkinson, March 13, 1789, quoted in ibid., 15.
4. For useful introductions to the history of the Democratic Party to 1860, see Richard E. Ellis, "Democratic Party, 1800–28," in *The Concise Princeton Encyclopedia of American Political History*, ed. Michael Kazin (Princeton, N.J.: Princeton University Press, 2011), 155–59; John Ashworth, "The Democratic Party, 1828–60," in ibid., 159–62; and Joel H. Silbey, "Democratic Party," in *The Political Lincoln: An Encyclopedia*, ed. Paul Finkleman and Martin J. Hershock (Washington, D.C.: CQ Press, 2009), 206–9. See also Sean Wilentz, *The Rise of American Democracy: Jefferson to Lincoln* (New York: W. W. Norton, 2005). The political culture of Northern Democrats in mid-nineteenth-century America is covered by Jean H. Baker, *Affairs of Party: The Political Culture of Northern Democrats in the Mid-Nineteenth Century* (Ithaca, N.Y.: Cornell University Press, 1983).
5. The history of the Whig Party can be found in William G. Shade, "Whig Party," in *Concise Princeton Encyclopedia of American Political History*,

600–603; Lawrence Frederick Kohl, "Whig Party," in *The Political Lincoln*, 707–10; Michael Holt, *The Rise and Fall of the American Whig Party: Jacksonian Politics and the Onset of the Civil War* (New York: Oxford University Press, 2003); and Daniel Walker Howe, *The Political Culture of the American Whigs* (Chicago: University of Chicago Press, 1979).

6. Daniel Walker Howe, *What Hath God Wrought: The Transformation of America, 1815–1848* (New York: Oxford University Press, 2007), 5.

7. For the role of almanacs in the American Revolution, see Marion Barber Stowell, "Revolutionary Almanac-Makers: Trumpeters of Sedition," *Papers of the Bibliographical Society of America* 73 (1979): 41–61; and Allan R. Raymond, "To Reach Men's Minds: Almanacs and the American Revolution," *New England Quarterly* 51 (1978): 370–95. For the role of pamphlets in the Revolution, see Bernard Bailyn, ed., *Pamphlets of the American Revolution, 1750–1776* (Cambridge, Mass.: Harvard University Press, 1965); Bernard Bailyn, *The Ideological Origins of the American Revolution* (Cambridge, Mass.: Harvard University Press, 1967), chapter 1. Newspapers and the Revolution are covered in Thomas C. Leonard, *The Power of the Press: The Birth of American Political Reporting* (New York: Oxford University Press, 1986), chapter 2; and Bernard Bailyn and John B. Hench, eds. *The Press and the American Revolution* (Boston: Northeastern University Press, 1981).

8. John Bidwell, "Printers' Supplies and Capitalization," in *The Colonial Book in the Atlantic World*, vol. 1 of *A History of the Book in America*, ed. Hugh Amory and David D. Hall (Worcester, Mass.: American Antiquarian Society, 2000), 163–64; James N. Green, "English Books and Printing in the Age of Franklin," in ibid., 266.

9. Leonard, *The Power of the Press*, 17–18. See also Charles E. Clark, *The Public Prints: The Newspaper in Anglo-American Culture* (New York: Oxford University Press, 1994).

10. Robert A. Gross, "An Extensive Republic," in *An Extensive Republic: Print, Culture, and Society in the New Nation, 1790–1840*, vol. 2 of *A History of the Book in America*, ed. Robert A. Gross and Mary Kelley (Chapel Hill: University of North Carolina Press, 2010), 18. The rise of the publishing industry in the new nation is discussed in James N. Green, "The Rise of Book Publishing," ibid., 75–127. On the creation of the American postal system and its impact on printing and publishing, see Richard John, *Spreading the News: The American Postal System from Franklin to Morse* (Cambridge, Mass.: Harvard University Press, 1996).

11. On the "reading revolution" in America, see Robert A. Gross, "Reading for an Extensive Republic," in Gross and Kelley, *An Extensive Republic*, 516–44; Cathy N. Davidson, *Revolution and the Word: The Rise of the Novel in America* (New York: Oxford University Press, 1986); William

J. Gilmore, *Reading Becomes a Necessity of Life: Material and Cultural Life in Rural New England, 1780–1835* (Knoxville: University of Tennessee Press, 1989); and David D. Hall, "The Uses of Literacy in New England, 1600–1850," in *Printing and Society in Early America*, ed. William L. Joyce, David D. Hall, Richard D. Brown, and John B. Hench (Worcester, Mass.: American Antiquarian Society, 1983). Hall surveys scholarship on this subject up to 1993 in "Readers and Reading in America: Historical and Critical Perspectives," *Proceedings of the American Antiquarian Society* 103 (1993): 337–58. The idea that nineteenth-century America was a unified nation of readers, however, is challenged by Ronald J. Zboray in *A Fictive People: Antebellum Economic Development and the American Reading Public* (New York: Oxford University Press, 1993). Davidson qualifies her initial support for an American "reading revolution" in "Towards a History of Books and Readers," in *Reading in America: Literature and Social History*, ed. Cathy N. Davidson (Baltimore: Johns Hopkins University Press, 1989), 14–18. Studies in literacy rates and reading skills have concentrated on colonial America, especially New England. See, for example, E. Jennifer Monaghan, *Learning to Read and Write in Colonial America* (Amherst and Boston: University of Massachusetts Press, 2005); Ross W. Beales and E. Jennifer Monaghan, "Literacy and Schoolbooks," in *The Colonial Book in the Atlantic World*, 380–86; and Jill Lepore, "Literacy and Reading in Puritan New England," in *Perspectives on Book History: Artifacts and Commentary*, ed. Scott E. Casper, Joanne D. Chaison, and Jeffrey D. Groves (Amherst and Boston: University of Massachusetts Press, 2002), 17–46. For the connection between education, personal self-improvement, and literacy in nineteenth-century America, see Gerald F. Moran and Maris A. Vinovskis, "Schools," in *An Extensive Republic*, 287–95; Scott E. Casper, "Introduction," in *The Industrial Book, 1840–1880*, vol. 3 of *A History of the Book in America*, ed. Scott E. Casper, Jeffrey D. Groves, Stephen W. Nissenbaum, and Michael Winship (Chapel Hill: University of North Carolina Press, 2007), 30–34; and Richard D. Brown, *Knowledge Is Power: The Diffusion of Information in Early America, 1700–1865* (New York: Oxford University Press, 1989), 228–29, 287.

12. James N. Green, "The Rise of Book Publishing," in Gross and Kelley, *An Extensive Republic*, 75–127, and "From Printer to Publisher: Mathew Carey and the Origins of Nineteenth-Century Book Publishing," in *Getting the Books Out: Papers of the Chicago Conference on the Book in 19th Century America*, ed. Michael Hackenberg (Washington, D.C.: Library of Congress, 1987), 26–44. On the numbers of publishing firms, booksellers, and printing houses in mid-nineteenth-century America,

see Candy Gunther Brown, *The Word in the World: Evangelical Writing, Publishing, and Reading in America, 1789–1880* (Chapel Hill: University of North Carolina Press, 2004), 47.

13. Rosalind Remer, *Printers and Men of Capital: Philadelphia Book Publishers in the New Republic* (Philadelphia: University of Pennsylvania Press, 1996), 100–124. See also Zboray, *A Fictive People.*
14. Charles Sellers, *The Market Revolution: Jacksonian America, 1815–1846* (New York: Oxford University Press, 1991); Melvyn Stokes and Stephen Conway, eds., *The Market Revolution in America: Social, Political, and Religious Expressions, 1800–1880* (Charlottesville: University Press of Virginia, 1996); "A Symposium on Charles Sellers, *The Market Revolution: Jacksonian America, 1815–1846,*" *Journal of the Early Republic* 12 (Winter 1992): 445–76; and John Larson, "The Market Revolution," in *A Companion to the Civil War and Reconstruction*, ed. Lacy K. Ford (West Sussex, UK: Wiley-Blackwell, 2011), 41–59. On the intensely competitive world of early American publishing, see Remer, *Printers and Men of Capital*, 100–124. On the emergence of the middle-class in America, see Stuart M. Blumin, *The Emergence of the Middle-Class: Social Experience in the American City, 1760–1900* (New York: Cambridge University Press, 1989); Burton J. Bledstein, *The Culture of Professionalism: The Middle Class and the Development of Higher Education in America* (New York: W. W. Norton, 1976); Burton J. Bledstein and Robert D. Johnston, eds., *The Middling Sorts: Explorations in the History of the American Middle Class* (New York: Routledge, 2001).
15. Gross, "An Extensive Republic," 37–40; Audie Tucher, "Newspapers and Periodicals," in Gross and Kelley, *An Extensive Republic*, 399–408.
16. John L. Brooke, "To Be 'Read by the Whole People': Press, Party, and the Public Sphere in the United States, 1789–1840," *Proceedings of the American Antiquarian Society* 110 (2000): 64, 80–81. See also Jeffrey L. Pasley, *"The Tyranny of Printers": Newspaper Politics in the Early American Republic* (Charlottesville: University Press of Virginia, 2001), 19.
17. Jabez Hammond is quoted in Silbey, *The American Political Nation*, 54. See also Pasley, *"Tyranny of Printers,"* 5–6.
18. Brooke, "To Be 'Read by the Whole People,'" 81; and Tucher, "Newspapers and Periodicals," 402. See also Gerald J. Baldasty, "The Press and Politics in the Age of Jackson," *Journalism Monographs* 89 (August 1984): 1–28; and Mel Laracey, "The Presidential Newspaper: The Forgotten Way of Going Public," in *Speaking to the People: The Rhetorical Presidency in Historical Perspective*, ed. Richard J. Ellis (Amherst: University of Massachusetts Press, 1998), 66–86.
19. Donald B. Cole, *A Jackson Man: Amos Kendall and the Rise of American Democracy* (Baton Rouge: Louisiana State University Press, 2004);

Louis A. Warren, "Raymond's Lincoln Books," *Lincoln Lore* 848 (July 9, 1945); Henry J. Raymond, *History of the Administration of President Lincoln: Including His Speeches, Letters, Addresses, Proclamations, and Messages* (New York: J. C. Derby and N. C. Miller, 1864); Mitchell Snay, *Horace Greeley and the Politics of Reform in Nineteenth-Century America* (Lanham, Md.: Rowman and Littlefield, 2011). See also Gregory A. Borchard, *Abraham Lincoln and Horace Greeley* (Carbondale and Edwardsville: Southern Illinois University Press, 2011).

20. Mark E. Neely Jr., *The Boundaries of American Political Culture in the Civil War Era* (Chapel Hill: University of North Carolina Press, 2005), 5.

21. Ibid., 2. Glen C. Altschuler and Stuart M. Blumin, in *Rude Republic: Americans and Their Politics in the Nineteenth Century* (Princeton, N.J.: Princeton University Press, 2000), argue that high voter turnouts in nineteenth-century elections did not mean that Americans were as actively engaged in the political process as some historians have maintained.

22. Tucher, "Newspapers and Periodicals," 407–8; Brooke, "To Be 'Read by the Whole People,'" 89. See also Robert Gray Gunderson, *The Log Cabin Campaign* (Lexington: University Press of Kentucky, 1957). For campaign newspapers, see William Miles, comp., *The People's Voice: An Annotated Bibliography of American Presidential Campaign Newspapers, 1828–1984* (Westport, Conn.: Greenwood, 1987).

23. Joel H. Silbey, ed., *The American Party Battle: Election Campaign Pamphlets, 1828–1876*, 2 vols. (Cambridge, Mass.: Harvard University Press, 1999), 1: xi–xvii. See also Bailyn, *Pamphlets of the American Revolution*.

24. Miles, *The People's Voice*, ix–x, 127. Both the Chicago and Cincinnati editions of *The Rail Splitter* were published in facsimile editions in 1950 by the Abraham Lincoln Bookshop in Chicago and now are available online in digital format.

25. Bryan F. Le Beau, *Currier & Ives: America Imagined* (Washington, D.C.: Smithsonian Institution Press, 2001), 6–7, 257–58; Neely, *The Boundaries of American Political Culture*, 9–16.

26. For an introduction to presidential campaign sheet music, see Danny O. Crew, *Presidential Sheet Music: An Illustrated Catalogue* (Jefferson, N.C.: McFarland, 2001), 1–32. *Tippecanoe Waltz* (Troy, N.Y.: A. Backus, 1840); *The Log Cabin Quick Step* (Baltimore: George Willig Jr., 1840); *Tippecanoe Hornpipe* (Baltimore: F. D. Benteen, 1840); *Honest Old Abe* (Buffalo: Blodgett and Bradford, 1860); *Lincoln Grand March* (Cincinnati: F. W. Rauch, 1860); *Lincoln Polka* (Cincinnati: J. Church, 1860).

27. Crew, *Presidential Sheet Music*, 1–32. *Harrison Melodies* (Boston: Weeks, Jordan & Co., 1840); *The Rough and Ready Songster* (New York: Nafis & Cornish, 1848).

28. Neely, *The Boundaries of American Political Culture*, 47–52. See also Frank Weitenkampf, *A Century of American Political Cartoons* (New York: Charles Scribner's Sons, 1944).
29. John Nerone, "Newspapers and the Public Sphere," in *The Industrial Book*, 239–41; Neely, *The Boundaries of American Political Culture*, 19–20.
30. Second Lecture of Discoveries and Inventions [February 11, 1859], *CW*, 3: 362. On the educational foundations of Lincoln's career, see Frank J. Williams, "The Educated Mr. Lincoln," in *The Living Lincoln*, ed. Thomas A. Horrocks, Harold Holzer, and Frank J. Williams (Carbondale and Edwardsville: Southern Illinois University Press, 2011), 9–19.
31. The statement "Public opinion in this country is everything" is from a Speech at Columbus, Ohio, September 16, 1859, *CW*, 3:424. The other quote is from Portion of a Speech at Republican Banquet in Chicago, Illinois, December 10, 1856, in Abraham Lincoln, *Speeches and Writings 1832–1858* (New York: Library of America, 1989), 385.
32. Michael Burlingame, "Lincoln Spins the Press," in *Lincoln Reshapes the Presidency*, ed. Charles M. Hubbard (Macon, Ga.: Mercer University Press, 2003), 65; Richard Carwardine, "Abraham Lincoln and the Fourth Estate: The White House and the Press during the American Civil War," *American Nineteenth Century History* 7 (March 2006): 3; Leonard, *The Power of the Press*, 93; Harold Holzer, "Lincoln and the Press: A Wary, Sometimes Testy, Relationship," in *Lincoln in the Times: The Life of Abraham Lincoln as Originally Reported in the* New York Times, ed. David Herbert Donald and Harold Holzer (New York: St. Martin's Press, 2005), 10.
33. William C. Harris, *Lincoln's Rise to the Presidency* (Lawrence: University Press of Kansas, 2007), 23; Richard Lawrence Miller, *Lincoln and His World: Prairie Politician 1834–1842* (Mechanicsburg, Pa.: Stackpole Books, 2008), 360–65.
34. Burlingame, *Abraham Lincoln*, 1: 563–64; Carwardine, "Abraham Lincoln and the Fourth Estate," 5; Contract with Theodore Canisius, May [?], 1859, *CW*, 3: 383–84; Reinhard H. Luthin, *The First Lincoln Campaign* (Cambridge, Mass.: Harvard University Press, 1944), 83. On German Americans and politics in mid-nineteenth-century America, see James M. Bergquist, "The Forty-Eighters: Catalysts of German-American Politics," in *The German-American Encounter: Conflict and Cooperation between Two Cultures, 1800–2000,* ed. Frank Trommler and Elliott Shore, 22–36 (New York: Berghahn, 2001); and Bruce Levine, *The Spirit of 1848: German Immigrants, Labor Conflict, and the Coming of the Civil War* (Urbana: University of Illinois Press, 1992). On

Lincoln's relationship with immigrants and ethnic groups, see Jason H. Silverman, "'One of the principal replenishing streams': Lincoln and His Evolving Relationship with Immigrants and Ethnic Groups," *Lincoln Herald* 114 (Fall 2012): 159–77.

35. Allen C. Guelzo, *Lincoln and Douglas: The Debates That Defined America* (New York: Simon and Schuster, 2008), 305–6; Burlingame, *Abraham Lincoln*, 1: 554, 570–71.

36. Harold Holzer, *Lincoln at Cooper Union: The Speech That Made Abraham Lincoln President* (New York: Simon and Schuster, 2004), 154, 224. For sales figures, see Bruce Chadwick, *Lincoln for President: An Unlikely Candidate, an Audacious Strategy, and the Victory No One Saw Coming* (Naperville, Ill.: Sourcebooks, 2009), 263.

37. Carwardine, "Abraham Lincoln and the Fourth Estate," 5–6; Laracey, "The Presidential Newspaper," 83–85; *National Intelligencer*, August 23, 1862; To Horace Greeley, August 22, 1862, *CW* 5: 388–89.

38. Mark E. Neely Jr., *The Fate of Liberty: Abraham Lincoln and Civil Liberties* (New York: Oxford University Press, 1991), 28–29. See also Robert Harper, *Lincoln and the Press* (New York: McGraw-Hill, 1951).

39. Harold Holzer, "The Campaign of 1860: Cooper Union, Mathew Brady, and the Campaign of Words and Images," in *Lincoln Revisited: New Insights from the Lincoln Forum*, ed. John Y. Simon, Harold Holzer, and Dawn Vogel (New York: Fordham University Press, 2007), 63–65; Holzer, *Lincoln at Cooper Union*, 100. See also Carole Payne, "Seeing Lincoln: Visual Encounters, in *The Cambridge Companion to Abraham Lincoln*, ed. Shirley Samuels (Cambridge: Cambridge University Press, 2012): 40–58.

2. Constructing the Ideal Candidate: Campaign Biographies and Image Making

1. To Jesse W. Fell, December 20, 1859, *CW*, 3: 511. For background on Fell's interest in Lincoln's life story, see Harold K. Sage, "Jesse W. Fell and the Lincoln Autobiography," *Journal of the Abraham Lincoln Association* 3 (1981): 49–59. Fell's remarks to Lincoln concerning the latter's growing reputation is cited in Guelzo, *Lincoln and Douglas*, 303. Fell served for a time as secretary of the Illinois Republican Party and later became the great-grandfather of Adlai Stevenson. Jean Baker, *"Not Much of Me": Abraham Lincoln as a Typical American* (Fort Wayne, Ind.: Louis A. Warren Lincoln Library and Museum, 1988).

2. *CW*, 3: 511; Sage, "Jesse W. Fell," 50–51; *Lincoln's Kalamazoo Address against Extending Slavery. Also His Life, by Joseph J. Lewis. Both Annotated by Thomas I. Starr* (Detroit: Fine Book Circle, 1941), 48–49.

3. *Lincoln's Kalamazoo Address*, 54–57, 60.

4. Michael Green, *Lincoln and the Election of 1860*, 77–87.
5. The Republican platform is discussed in Burlingame, *Abraham Lincoln*, 1: 611–13.
6. *Chicago Rail Splitter*, July 7, 1860; *Cincinnati Rail Splitter*, August 1 and 8, 1860; *Honest Old Abe*; William H. Burleigh, ed., *The Republican Campaign Songster for 1860* (New York: H. Dayton, 1860), 45. Only representative stanzas of the *Harrah for Lincoln* are cited.
7. *Chicago Rail Splitter*, July 1, 1860. On Lincoln's association with the West, see Richard W. Etulain, "Abraham Lincoln and the Trans-Mississippi American West: An Introductory Overview," in *Lincoln Looks West: From the Mississippi to the Pacific*, ed. Richard W. Etulain (Carbondale and Edwardsville: Southern Illinois University Press, 2010), 1–67.
8. Burleigh, *The Republican Campaign Songster for 1860*, 10–11. Only representative stanzas are quoted.
9. Almon H. Benedict, *A "Wide-Awake" Poem* (Cortland Village, N.Y.: 1860) quoted in Patricia Hochwalt Wynne, "Lincoln's Western Image in the 1860 Campaign," *Maryland Historical Magazine* 59 (1964): 169.
10. *New York Daily Tribune*, May 21, 1860, quoted in ibid., 167. See also Borchard, *Abraham Lincoln and Horace Greeley*.
11. Criticisms leveled at Jackson during the 1828 campaign are discussed in Donald B. Cole, *Vindicating Andrew Jackson: The 1828 Election and the Rise of the Two-Party System* (Lawrence: University Press of Kansas, 2009). Lincoln's war record was criticized by the *New York Herald*, July 9, 1860; Lincoln as a "third-rate lawyer" appears in the *Union Democrat* (Manchester, New Hampshire), no date given. Both are cited in Wynne, "Lincoln's Western Image," 176, 178.
12. *Philadelphia Evening Journal* article is reprinted in the *New York Semi-Weekly Tribune*, May 25, 1860 and cited in Wynne, "Lincoln's Western Image," 178.
13. *Boston Semi-Weekly Courier*, May 21, 1860.
14. *Boston Daily Advertiser*, May 21, 1860.
15. *New York Daily Tribune*, May 24, 1860.
16. *New York Daily Tribune*, October 23, 1860, is cited in Mitgang, *Abraham Lincoln: A Press Portrait*, 199–200.
17. *Lincoln Quick Step* (Philadelphia: Lee & Walker, 1860); *The "Wigwam" Grand March* (Boston: Oliver Ditson & Co., 1860). For a useful review of the range of Lincoln images produced before for the election of 1860, see Harold Holzer, Gabor S. Boritt, and Mark E. Neely Jr., *The Lincoln Image: Abraham Lincoln and the Popular Print* (New York: Charles Scribner's Sons, 1984).
18. This advertisement is cited in Holzer, Boritt, and Neely, *The Lincoln Image*, 16–17; *The Republican Standard* (Chicago: Rufus Blanchard,

1860); *National Republican Chart/Presidential Campaign, 1860* (New York: H. H. Lloyd, 1860). Lloyd's advertisement is cited in Harold Holzer, Gabor S. Boritt, and Mark E. Neely Jr., *Changing the Lincoln Image* (Fort Wayne, Ind.: Louis A. Warren Lincoln Library and Museum, 1985), 32.
19. *Momus* (New York), June 2, 1860 is cited in Gary L. Bunker, *From Rail-Splitter to Icon: Lincoln's Image in Illustrated Periodicals, 1860–1865* (Kent, Ohio: Kent State University Press, 2001), 35.
20. *The Rail Candidate* (New York: Currier & Ives, 1860); *"The Nigger" in the Woodpile* (New York: Currier & Ives, 1860).
21. One example is Susan B. Anthony's call for the inauguration of "Abram Lincoln," and another is the declaration of the *Albany (N.Y.) Evening Journal* that "Abram Lincoln" was its choice for president. Both are cited in Egerton, *Year of Meteors*, 15, 129.
22. John Henry Eaton, *The Life of Andrew Jackson, Major-General in the Service of the United States; Comprising a History of the War in the South from the Commencement of the Creek Campaign, to the Termination of Hostilities before New Orleans* (Philadelphia: Samuel Bradford, 1824). Useful sources for American presidential campaign biographies are W. Burlie Brown, *The People's Choice: The Presidential Image in the Campaign Biography* (Baton Rouge: Louisiana State University Press, 1960); M. J. Heale, *The Presidential Quest: Candidates and Images in American Political Culture, 1787–1852* (London and New York: Longman, 1982); and Scott E. Casper, *Constructing American Lives: Biography and Culture in Nineteenth-Century America* (Chapel Hill: University of North Carolina Press, 1999), 94–97. An essential source is William Miles, *The Image Makers: A Bibliography of American Presidential Campaign Biographies* (Metuchen, N.J.: Scarecrow Press, 1979). See also Jill Lepore, "Bound for Glory," *New Yorker*, October 20, 2008, 80–85.
23. Scott E. Casper, *Constructing American Lives*, 95–96; Brown, *The People's Choice*, 5–7.
24. Brown, *The People's Choice*, 12; Heale, *The Presidential Quest*, 159–60.
25. Brown, *The People's Choice*, 9. Nathaniel Hawthorne's biography was entitled *Life of Franklin Pierce* (Boston: Ticknor, Reeds, and Fields, 1852). It is not clear which biography of Scott is referred to in the citation.
26. Brown, *The People's Choice*, 9–10. Brown's quote is from Ernest James Wessen, "Campaign Lives of Abraham Lincoln, 1860: An Annotated Bibliography of the Biographies of Abraham Lincoln Issued during the Campaign Year," *Papers in Illinois History* (1938): 188. Scott E. Casper, "The Two Lives of Franklin Pierce: Hawthorne, Political Culture, and

the Literary Market," *American Literary History* 5 (Summer 1993): 211, 215. Charles Wentworth Upham, *Life, Explorations and Public Services of John Charles Frémont* (Boston: Ticknor and Fields, 1856). The two Harrison biographies published by Boston's Weeks, Jordan & Co. are Caleb Cushing, *Outlines of the Life and Public Services, Civil and Military, of William Henry Harrison* (Boston: Weeks, Jordan & Co., 1840); and Richard Hildreth, *The People's Candidate; or, The Life of William Henry Harrison of Ohio* (Boston: Weeks, Jordan & Co., 1839).

27. See, for example, *The Life of Major-General William Henry Harrison: Comprising a Brief Account of His Important Civil and Military Services* (Philadelphia: Grigg & Elliott, 1840); and *Life and Public Services of Gen. Z. Taylor . . . With Fifteen Illustrations . . .* (New York: E. Hutchinson, 1848).
28. Casper, *Constructing American Lives*, 4, 6, 10.
29. Ibid., 43, 81, 95, 97–98.
30. Brown, *The People's Choice*, 17–20; Heale, *The Presidential Quest*, 162–63.
31. Brown, *The People's Choice*, 29–30.
32. Ibid., 48–58.
33. Ibid., 65–74; Heale, *The Presidential Quest*, 166–67.
34. Brown, *The People's Choice*, 83–97.
35. Ibid., 104–12.
36. Ibid., 125–32.
37. Ibid., 135.

3. Promoting Honest Abe, the Rail Splitter: Lincoln's 1860 Campaign Biographies

1. William E. Barton, "The Lincoln of the Biographers," *Transactions of the Illinois State Historical Society* 36 (1929): 64; *Erie (Pa.) True American*, May 26, 1860, cited in *Lincoln Lore* (May 12, 1930).
2. There is no evidence that W. A. Townsend ever published a campaign biography of Lincoln. See Wessen, "Campaign Lives of Abraham Lincoln"; and Miles, *The Image Makers*.
3. "Hon. Abram Lincoln, of Illinois. Republican Candidate for President," *Harper's Weekly*, May 26, 1860. The author used this version of this biographical account. A shorter version of the sketch, upon which the *Harper's Weekly* account is based, appeared in Horace Greeley's *New York Daily Tribune* on May 19 under the title "Honest Old Abe."
4. Form Letter to Applicants for Biographical Data [June] 1860, *CW*, 4: 60.
5. *The Life, Speeches, and Public Services of Abram Lincoln, together with a Sketch of the Life of Hannibal Hamlin* (New York: Rudd & Carleton, 1860); Barton, "The Lincoln of the Biographers," 66; Wessen, "Campaign Lives of Abraham Lincoln," 192; *Lincoln Lore* (September

30, 1940); Miles, *The Image Makers*, 68. George W. Carleton (1832–1901) was the primary owner of Rudd & Carleton. The partnership lasted for a brief period, from 1857 to Rudd's death in late 1860 or 1861. Carleton remained in the publishing business through the 1860s before retiring. John Tebbel, *A History of Book Publishing in the United States*, vol. 1: *The Creation of an Industry, 1630–1865* (New York: R. R. Bowker, 1972), 343–49.

6. D. W. Bartlett, *The Life and Public Services of Hon. Abraham Lincoln* (New York: H. Dayton, 1860) and *The Life and Public Services of Hon. Abraham Lincoln*, "Authorized" 2nd ed. (New York: H. Dayton, 1860); Wessen, "Campaign Lives of Abraham Lincoln," 192–94. Bartlett's obituary appeared in the *New York Times,* June 26, 1912. No information was found on the publishing firm of H. Dayton. J. C. Derby, an Auburn, New York, publisher, moved to New York City in 1853 and formed a partnership with Edwin Jackson in 1855. The partnership lasted until 1861. The firm specialized in American and English literature. Tebbel, *A History of Book Publishing in the United States*, 1: 342–43. Although active in the Whig Party in the 1840s, Derby appeared to be politically neutral when it came to his publishing activities. J. C. Derby, *Fifty Years among Authors, Books and Publishers* (New York: G. W. Carleton & Co., 1884), 21–48.

7. D. W. Bartlett, *The Life and Public Services of Hon. Abraham Lincoln . . . to which is added a Biographical Sketch of Hon. Hannibal Hamlin*, rev. ed. (New York: H. Dayton, 1860); Wessen, "Campaign Lives of Abraham Lincoln," 200–201.

8. [R. J. Hinton], *The Life and Public Services of Hon. Abraham Lincoln, of Illinois, and Hon. Hannibal Hamlin, of Maine* (Boston: Thayer & Eldridge, 1860); *The Life and Public Services of Hon. Abraham Lincoln, of Illinois, and Hon. Hannibal Hamlin, of Maine*, 2nd ed. (Boston: Thayer & Eldridge, 1860); *The Life and Public Services of Hon. Abraham Lincoln, of Illinois, and Hon. Hannibal Hamlin, of Maine*, "Wide Awake" edition (Boston: Thayer & Eldridge, 1860); Barton, "The Lincoln of the Biographers," 65; Wessen, "Campaign Lives of Abraham Lincoln," 195–97, 201–202; *Political Debates between Hon. Abraham Lincoln and Hon. Stephen A. Douglas* (Columbus, Ohio: Follett, Foster & Co., 1860); Lloyd Ostendorf, *Lincoln's Photographs: A Complete Album* (Dayton, Ohio: Rockwood Press, 1998), 20. Information on Thayer and Eldridge, as well as Hinton, can be found in Albert J. Von Frank, "The Secret World of Radical Publishers: The Case of Thayer and Eldridge of Boston," in *Boston's Histories: Essays in Honor of Thomas H. O'Connor*, ed. James M. O'Toole and David Quigley (Boston: Northeastern University Press, 2004), 52–76. Biographical details on Hinton's life can be found

in C. Carroll Hollis, "R. J. Hinton: Lincoln's Reluctant Biographer," *Centennial Review* 50 (1961): 65–84; and "Richard Josiah Hinton" in www.kansasmemory.org/item/213201 (accessed May 25, 2013).

9. E. B. Washburne, *Abraham Lincoln, His Personal History and Public Record* (Washington, D.C.: Republican Congressional Committee, 1860); Washburne remarks to Lincoln cited in Mark E. Neely Jr., *The Abraham Lincoln Encyclopedia* (New York: Da Capo Press, 1982), 323; Wessen, "Campaign Lives of Abraham Lincoln," 197. John Y. Simon, "Washburne, Elihu Benjamin," *American National Biography Online* Feb. 2000. http://www.anb.org/articles/04/04-01038.html (Accessed May 28, 2013).

10. Ichabod Codding, *A Republican Manual for the Campaign. Facts for the People: The Whole Argument in One Book* (Princeton, Ill.: "Republican" Book and Job Printing Office, 1860); Wessen, "Campaign Lives of Abraham Lincoln," 198; Neely, *Abraham Lincoln Encyclopedia*, 61. According to a 1962 issue of *Lincoln Lore*, only seven copies of Codding's work were known to exist. See [Gerald McMurtry], "Codding's 'Republican Manual for the Campaign—1860,'" *Lincoln Lore* 1490 (April 1962). Wessen, see above, speculates that this publication was suppressed by the Republican Party. For information on Codding and his relationship with Lincoln, see Neely, *Abraham Lincoln Encyclopedia*, 61; and Allen C. Guelzo, "'Fiends . . . Facing Zionwards': Abraham Lincoln's Reluctant Embrace of the Abolitionists," *Abraham Lincoln as a Man of Ideas* (Carbondale: Southern Illinois University Press, 2009), 97.

11. Reuben Vose, *The Life and Speeches of Abraham Lincoln, and Hannibal Hamlin* (New York: Reuben Vose, 1860); Wessen, "Campaign Lives of Abraham Lincoln," 198–99; [L. Warren], "Vose's Lincoln," *Lincoln Lore* 419 (April 19, 1937).

12. Robert Price, "Young Howells Drafts a 'Life' for Lincoln," *Ohio History* 76 (1998): 232–33.

13. William Dean Howells, *Years of My Youth* (New York: Harper & Brothers, 1916), 202.

14. John G. Nicolay to Messrs. Follett & Foster, June 15, 1860; John G. Nicolay to James Q. Howard, June 19, 1860, in Michael Burlingame, ed., *With Lincoln in the White House: Letters, Memoranda, and Other Writings of John G. Nicolay, 1860–1865* (Carbondale and Edwardsville: Southern Illinois University Press, 2000), 2–3; Lincoln to Samuel Galloway, June 19, 1860, *CW*, 4: 79–80; Wessen, "Campaign Lives of Abraham Lincoln," 209.

15. [W. D. Howells], *Lives and Speeches of Abraham Lincoln and Hannibal Hamlin* (Columbus, Ohio: Follett, Foster & Co., 1860); Wessen, "Campaign Lives of Abraham Lincoln," 209. Lincoln's corrected copy

of Howells's biography was published in 1938 in Springfield, Illinois, by the Abraham Lincoln Association. Howells, *Years of My Youth*, 203.
16. Wessen, "Campaign Lives of Abraham Lincoln," 207.
17. Neely, *Abraham Lincoln Encyclopedia*, 152.
18. J. H. Barrett, *Life of Abraham Lincoln (of Illinois). With a Condensed View of His Most Important Speeches; also a Sketch of the Life of Hannibal Hamlin (of Maine)* (Cincinnati: Moore, Wilstach, Keys & Co., 1860); Wessen, "Campaign Lives of Abraham Lincoln," 206. Barrett's relationship with Lincoln is discussed in Joseph R. Nightingale, "Lincoln's Friend and Biographer: Joseph Hartwell Barrett," *Journal of the Illinois State Historical Society* 96 (2003): 206–28. Preceded and succeeded by several incarnations, Moore, Wilstach, Keys & Co. was established in 1855 and soon became Cincinnati's largest general publishing firm. Issuing publications on a variety of subjects, including literature, history, medicine, music, and juvenile adventure stories, the partnership disbanded in 1869. There is no indication that the partnership was politically active in supporting the Republican Party in general or Lincoln in particular. Walter Sutton, *The Western Book Trade: Cincinnati as a Nineteenth-Century Publishing and Book-Trade Center* (Columbus: Ohio State University Press, 1961), 118–27.
19. John L. Scripps to William Henry Herndon, in Douglas L. Wilson and Rodney O. Davis, ed., *Herndon's Informants: Letters, Interviews, and Statements about Abraham Lincoln* (Urbana and Chicago: University of Illinois Press, 1998), 57.
20. Autobiography written for John L. Scripps, [June 1860], *CW*, 4: 60–67.
21. Burlingame, *Abraham Lincoln*, 1: 648 (including Scripps's quote); Joseph R. Nightingale, "Joseph H. Barrett and John Locke Scripps, Shapers of Lincoln's Religious Image," *Journal of the Illinois State Historical Society* (Autumn 1999), 13.
22. [John Locke Scripps], *Life of Abraham Lincoln* (Chicago: *Chicago Press and Tribune*, 1860), and *Tribune Tracts, No 6: Life of Abraham Lincoln* (New York: Horace Greeley & Co., 1860); Barton, "The Lincoln of the Biographers," 91; Wessen, "Campaign Lives of Abraham Lincoln," 211–13. Single copies of Scripps's biography of Lincoln sold for five cents, while a dozen sold for forty cents, a hundred copies sold for three dollars and fifty cents, and a thousand copies sold for twenty dollars.
23. Scripps, *Life of Lincoln* (*Chicago Press and Tribune* edition), 3; Scripps's remarks to Lincoln are cited in Egerton, *Year of Meteors*, 180. Sale figures for Scripps's biography come from Stephen B. Oates, *With Malice toward None: The Life of Abraham Lincoln* (New York: Harper

& Row, 1977), 181. On Scripps's appointment as postmaster, see Neely, *Abraham Lincoln Encyclopedia*, 271.
24. J. Q. Howard, *The Life of Abraham Lincoln: With Extracts from His Speeches* (Columbus: Follett, Foster & Co.; Cincinnati: Anderson, Gates & Wright, 1860), and *Das Leben von Abraham Lincoln, nebst Auszugen aus seinen Reden. Aus dem Englischen von J. Q. Howard, Uebersezt druch Professor Wilhelm Grauert* (Columbus: Follett, Foster & Co., 1860); Miles, *The Image Makers*, 66; Wessen, "Campaign Lives of Abraham Lincoln," 214; Barton, "The Lincoln of the Biographers," 90.
25. William Henry Fry, *Republican "Campaign" Text-Book, for the Year 1860* (New York: A. B. Burdick, 1860); Barbara L. Tischler, "Fry, William Henry," *American National Biography Online,* Feb. 2000. http://www.anb.org/articles/18/18-00425.html (Accessed May 28, 2013).
26. *Wells' Illustrated National Campaign Hand-Book for 1860* (New York: J. G. Wells; Cincinnati: Mack R. Barnitz, 1860).
27. *The Lives of the Present Candidates for President and Vice-President of the United States, Containing a Condensed and Impartial History of the Lives, Public Acts, and Political Views of the Present Candidates, with Platforms of the Parties they Represent, Their Portraits from Life, Their Letters of Acceptance, etc.* (Cincinnati: H. M. Rulison; Philadelphia: D. Rulison; St. Louis: C. Drew & Co.; Geneva, N.Y.: J. Whitley Jr., 1860). For information on the photograph on which the woodcut was based, see Lloyd Ostendorf, *Lincoln's Photographs: A Complete Album* (Dayton, Ohio: Rockywood Press, 1998), 28–29.
28. *Portraits and Sketches of the Lives of all the Candidates for the Presidency and Vice-Presidency, for 1860* (New York: J. C. Buttre, 1860).
29. To Jesse W. Fell, Enclosing Autobiography, December 20, 1859, *CW*, 3: 511.
30. *The Life, Speeches, and Public Services of Abram Lincoln*, 7.
31. Vose, *The Life and Speeches of Abraham Lincoln*, iii; Barrett, *Life of Abraham Lincoln*, 11.
32. *Illustrated National Campaign Hand-Book*, 45; *Lives of the Present Candidates for President and Vice President*, 44.
33. *The Life and Public Services of Hon. Abraham Lincoln*, 13; Howard, *The Life of Abraham Lincoln*, 3.
34. Autobiography Written for John L. Scripps, *CW*, 4:61–62.
35. Scripps, *Life of Lincoln*, 1.
36. The lack of educational opportunities available to Lincoln and others raised in similar circumstances is discussed in Myron Marty, "Schooling in Lincoln's America and Lincoln's Extraordinary Self-Schooling," in *Lincoln's America 1809–1865*, ed. Joseph F. Fornieri and Sara Vaughn Gabbard (Carbondale: Southern Illinois University Press, 2008), 55–71.

37. Howells, *Lives and Speeches of Abraham Lincoln*, 21; Howard, *The Life of Abraham Lincoln*, 5; Scripps, *Life of Lincoln*, 4.
38. Howells, *Lives and Speeches of Abraham Lincoln*, 20–21 [restless ambition]; Barrett, *Life of Abraham Lincoln,* 25.
39. Washburne, *Abraham Lincoln*, 1; Howard, *The Life of Abraham Lincoln*, 8.
40. Scripps, *Life of Lincoln*, 4: Barrett, *Life of Abraham Lincoln*, 24–25; 28–29.
41. *The Life and Public Services of Hon. Abraham Lincoln*, 14.
42. Barrett, *Life of Abraham Lincoln*, 25; Howard, *The Life of Abraham Lincoln*, 7–8; Scripps, *Life of Lincoln*, 3.
43. Scripps, *Life of Lincoln*, 4.
44. Howard, *The Life of Abraham Lincoln*, 18–19; Howells, *Lives and Speeches of Abraham Lincoln*, 35. The images of Lincoln's physical strength and aggressive masculinity conveyed by his biographers as well as through print media are discussed in Michael Thomas Smith, "Abraham Lincoln, Manhood, and Nineteenth-Century American Political Culture," in *This Distracted and Anarchical People: New Answers for Old Questions about the Civil War-Era North*, ed. Andrew L. Slap and Michael Thomas Smith (New York: Fordham University Press, 2013), 29–41.
45. *The Life and Public Services of Hon. Abraham Lincoln*, 10; Washburne, *Abraham Lincoln*, 2.
46. Barrett, *Life of Abraham Lincoln*, 45; *The Lives of the Present Candidates*, 48.
47. Howard, *The Life of Abraham Lincoln*, 13–14. See also Howells, *Lives and Speeches of Abraham Lincoln*, 38–39.
48. Scripps, *Life of Lincoln*, 6–7.
49. Autobiography Written for John L. Scripps, *CW*, 4: 65.
50. Howells, *Lives and Speeches of Abraham Lincoln*, 43.
51. Scripps, *Life of Lincoln*, 13; Bartlett, *The Life and Public Services of Hon. Abraham Lincoln*, 2nd "authorized" edition, 25; Howells, *Lives and Speeches of Abraham Lincoln*, 48.
52. Hinton, *The Life and Public Services of Hon. Abraham Lincoln*, 18–22; Barrett, *Life of Abraham Lincoln*, 63–66; Howells, *Lives and Speeches of Abraham Lincoln*, 35–36. See also John Evangelist Walsh, *Moonlight: Abraham Lincoln and the Almanac Trial* (New York: St. Martin's Press, 2000).
53. Barrett, *Life of Abraham Lincoln*, 55.
54. Scripps, *Life of Lincoln*, 15; Barrett, *Life of Abraham Lincoln*, 74.
55. Hinton, *The Life and Public Services of Hon. Abraham Lincoln*, 23; Bartlett, *The Life and Public Services of Hon. Abraham Lincoln*, 2nd ed., 60.
56. Barrett, *Life of Abraham Lincoln*, 69.
57. Hinton, *The Life and Public Services of Hon. Abraham Lincoln*, 28; Howard, *The Life of Abraham Lincoln*, 50.

58. Barrett, *Life of Abraham Lincoln*, 181; Bartlett, *The Life and Public Services of Hon. Abraham Lincoln*, 79–100; "fraudulent districting" appears in ibid., 89.
59. *Lincoln's Kalamazoo Address*, 63; Howard, *The Life of Abraham Lincoln*, 58.
60. Bartlett, *The Life and Public Services of Hon. Abraham Lincoln*, 106; Howells, *Lives and Speeches of Abraham Lincoln*, 93; Howard, *The Life of Abraham Lincoln*, 58.
61. Scripps, *Life of Lincoln*, 14; Barrett, *Life of Abraham Lincoln*, 67; Howells, *Lives and Speeches of Abraham Lincoln*, 53. Mary Lincoln's positive coverage by the press in 1860 is described in Catherine Clinton, *Mrs. Lincoln: A Life* (New York: HarperCollins, 2009), 110–12.
62. Handbill Replying to Charges of Infidelity, July 31, 1846, in *CW*, 1: 382.
63. Bartlett, *The Life and Public Services of Hon. Abraham Lincoln*, 106; Scripps, *Life of Lincoln*, 2; Howard, *The Life of Abraham Lincoln*, 58.
64. *The Life, Speeches, and Public Services of Abram Lincoln*, 6.
65. *The Life and Public Services of Hon. Abraham Lincoln*, 9; Scripps, *Life of Lincoln*, 31; Vose, *The Life and Speeches of Abraham Lincoln and Hannibal Hamlin*, ix–x.
66. Barrett, *Life of Abraham Lincoln*, 192; Howard, *The Life of Abraham Lincoln*, 59.
67. Howells, *Lives and Speeches of Abraham Lincoln*, 50.
68. Robert W. Johannsen, *Stephen A. Douglas* (Urbana and Chicago: University of Illinois Press, 1997), 701, 732–33; James A. Sheahan, *The Life of Stephen A. Douglas* (New York: Harper & Brothers, 1860). Sheahan's and Douglas's roles in founding the *Chicago Times* are found in "Chicago Times," in http://www.encyclopedia.chicagohistory.org/pages/216.html (Accessed May 28, 2013).
69. Johannsen, *Stephen A. Douglas*, 749–73; James L. Huston, "The 1860 Southern Sojourns of Stephen A. Douglas and the Irrepressible Separation," in Fuller, *The Election of 1860 Reconsidered*, 32–33; A. James Fuller, "A Forlorn Hope: Interpreting the Breckinridge Campaign as a Matter of Honor," in ibid., 71–72.
70. Johannsen, *Stephen A. Douglas*, 782–83; Egerton, *Year of Meteors*, 198–99; Huston, "The 1860 Southern Sojourns of Stephen A. Douglas," 29–67.
71. Egerton, *Year of Meteors*, 198–99.
72. [Henry M. Flint], *Life of Stephen A. Douglas, United States Senator from Illinois. With His Most Important Speeches and Reports* (New York: Derby & Jackson; Chicago: D. B. Cooke & Co., 1860); Robert B. Warden, *A Voter's Version of the Life and Character of Stephen Arnold Douglas* (Columbus: Follett, Foster & Co., 1860). The two pamphlets are *Biographical Sketch of Stephen A. Douglas* (Washington, 1860) and the

Life of Stephen A. Douglas, U.S. Senator from Illinois (Baltimore: John P. Des Forges, 1860). Chapters on Douglas appear in Wells, *Illustrated National Campaign Hand-Book for 1860*; *The Lives of the Present Candidates for President and Vice-President of the United States*; and *Portraits and Sketches of the Lives of all the Candidates for the Presidency and Vice-Presidency, for 1860*. The German biographical account is *Biographie von Stephan Arnold Douglas. Präsidentschafts-Candidaten der Americanischen Democratie. Herausgegeben von der National-Executiv-Committee* (New York: Office der "New-Yorker Staats-Zeitung," 1860). The publishing house of Harper, like Derby & Jackson and Follett, Foster & Co., appears to have been nonpartisan in its publishing activity. Tebbel, *A History of Publishing in the United States*, 1: 269–83.

73. *Lives of the Present Candidates for President and Vice President*, 101.
74. Fuller, "A Forlorn Hope," 97; William C. Davis, *Breckinridge: Statesman, Soldier, Symbol* (Lexington: University Press of Kentucky, 2010), 230, 233. Fuller claims that Breckinridge wanted the nomination of the Southern wing of the Democratic Party. Davis, on the other hand, portrays Breckinridge as a reluctant nominee.
75. *Biographical Sketches of Hon. John C. Breckinridge, Democratic Nominee for President, and General Joseph Lane, Democratic Nominee for Vice President* (Washington: National Democratic Executive Committee, 1860).
76. *Portraits and Sketches of John C. Breckinridge and Joseph Lane* (New York: J. C. Buttre, 1860); Wells, *Illustrated National Campaign Hand-Book for 1860*; *The Lives of the Present Candidates for President and Vice-President of the United States*; and *Portraits and Sketches of the Lives of all the Candidates for the Presidency and Vice-Presidency, for 1860*.
77. *Biographical Sketches of Hon. John C. Breckinridge*, 5.
78. Ibid., 18.
79. *Portraits and Sketches of John C. Breckinridge and Joseph Lane*, 5.
80. *The Life, Speeches, and Public Services of John Bell, together with a Sketch of the Life of Edward Everett. Union Candidates for the Offices of President and Vice-President, of the United States* (New York: Rudd & Carleton, 1860). The other three biographies are Wells, *Illustrated National Campaign Hand-Book for 1860*; *The Lives of the Present Candidates for President and Vice-President of the United States*; and *Portraits and Sketches of the Lives of all the Candidates for the Presidency and Vice-Presidency*.
81. *Lives of the Present Candidates for President and Vice President*, 18. Bell's 1860 campaign is covered in A. James Fuller, "The Last True Whig: John Bell and the Politics of Compromise in 1860," in Fuller, *The Election of 1860 Reconsidered*, 103–39.

82. Thomas A. Horrocks, "Abraham Lincoln, 16th President of the United States," in *Chronology of the U.S. Presidency*, ed. Matthew Manweller, 4 vols. (Santa Barbara: ABC-CLIO, 2012), 2:477. Green, *Lincoln and the Election of 1860*, 107.

4. The 1864 Campaign: The Rail Splitter as Father Abraham

1. Burlingame, *Abraham Lincoln*, 2: 627–40. The best study of the Copperheads is Jennifer L. Weber, *Copperheads: The Rise and Fall of Lincoln's Opponents in the North* (Oxford: Oxford University Press, 2006).
2. Burlingame, *Abraham Lincoln*, 2: 641–42; On Lincoln's use of patronage and cultivation of the press, see Richard Carwardine, *Lincoln* (London: Pearson Education Ltd., 2003), 263–66; and "Abraham Lincoln and the Fourth Estate." Lincoln's behind-the-scenes role in the Unionism as patriotism strategy, see Carwardine, *Lincoln*, 266–67. An excellent study of the political use of Unionism in the Civil War North is Adam I. P. Smith, *No Party Now: Politics in the Civil War North* (Oxford: Oxford University Press, 2006). See also Mark E. Neely Jr., *The Union Divided: Party Conflict in the Civil War North* (Cambridge, Mass.: Harvard University Press, 2002).
3. Stephen W. Sears, *George B. McClellan: The Young Napoleon* (New York: Ticknor and Fields, 1988), 371–74.
4. Raymond cited in Burlingame, *Abraham Lincoln*, 2: 669; Memorandum Concerning His Probable Failure of Re-election, August 24, 1864, *CW*: 7: 514.
5. The 1864 campaign is covered by Burlingame, *Abraham Lincoln*, 2: 681–730; David E. Long, *The Jewel of Liberty: Abraham Lincoln's Re-election and the End of Slavery* (Mechanicsburg, Penn.: Stackpole Books, 1994); and John C. Waugh, *Reelecting Lincoln: The Battle for the 1864 Presidency* (New York: Crown, 1997).
6. These figures are based on Miles, *The Image Makers*, 72–76. This author disagrees with several of the works Miles lists as Lincoln campaign biographies, some of which were published in 1863 and earlier.
7. Henry J. Raymond, *History of the Administration of President Lincoln*. The advertisement cited was bound into the copy of Raymond's work consulted by the author. One suspects that the National Union Party funded this publication. Raymond's preface is dated May 5, 1864, about a month prior to the National Union Party convention, indicating that it should have appeared on the market soon thereafter. Joseph Nightingale, in "Lincoln's Friend and Biographer: Joseph Hartwell Barrett," 206, states that Raymond's work was published on or about June 11, days after the convention. He provides no evidence for this claim, however.

8. Henry J. Raymond, *The Life of Abraham Lincoln . . . and of Andrew Johnson, by John Savage* (New York: National Union Executive Committee, 1864).
9. Joseph H. Barrett, *Life of Abraham Lincoln, presenting His Early History, Political Career, and Speeches in and out of Congress; also a General View of His Policy as President of the United States; with Messages, Proclamations, Letters, etc., and a Concise History of the War* (Cincinnati: Moore, Wilstach & Baldwin, 1864). Barrett's preface is dated May 14, 1864, indicating that the book should have appeared on the market soon thereafter. Nightingale, in "Lincoln's Friend and Biographer: Joseph Hartwell Barrett, 206, declares that Barrett's biography was published on June 18, but, again, provides no evidence to support this statement.
10. [David Brainerd Williamson], *The Life and Public Services of Abraham Lincoln, Sixteenth President of the United States; and Commander-in-Chief of the Army and Navy of the United States* (Philadelphia: T. B. Peterson & Brothers, 1864). The statement that this work was published prior to the National Union Party convention is found on page 179, which refers to the upcoming National Union Party convention. T. B. Peterson & Co. was formed in Philadelphia in 1858 and remained in business until 1890. Publishers of American and British fiction, especially Charles Dickens, Peterson & Co. appears to have been nonpartisan in their publishing activities. Tebbel, *A History of Book Publishing in the United States*, 1: 246–47; "Notes and Queries," *Pennsylvania Magazine of History and Biography* 36 (1912): 118–19.
11. O. J. Victor, *The Private and Public Life of Abraham Lincoln; comprising a Full Account of His Early Years, and a Succinct Record of His Career as Statesman and President* (New York: Beadle & Co., 1864); Barton, "The Lincoln of the Biographers," 70; JoAnn Castagna, "Victor, Orville James," *American National Biography Online* Feb. 2000. http://www.anb.org/articles/16/16-01697.html.
12. Abbott A. Abbott, *The Life of Abraham Lincoln* (New York: T. R. Dawley, 1864); [Union League of Philadelphia], *Address by The Union League of Philadelphia, to the Citizens of Pennsylvania, in Favor of the Re-Election of Abraham Lincoln* (Philadelphia: The Union League of Philadelphia, 1864); *A Workingman's Reasons for the Re-Election of Abraham Lincoln* (n.p., 1864); J. M. Hiatt, *The Political Manual, comprising Numerous Important Documents connected with the Political History of America, compiled from Official Records, with Biographical Sketches and Comments* (Indianapolis: Asher & Adams, 1864).
13. William M. Thayer, *The Character and Public Services of Abraham Lincoln, President of the United States* (Boston: Dinsmoor and Company, 1864). Walker, Wise, and Company was the other Boston publisher of Thayer's campaign biography. This firm, established in 1859, published

Unitarian works, children's books, and several titles on women's rights. The publishing house also issued political works, including speeches and lectures of the ardent abolitionist Wendell Phillips. Tebbel, *A History of Book Publishing in the United States*, 1: 432–33. Thayer's Lincoln book directed to adolescent boys was *The Pioneer Boy, and How He Became President* (Boston: Walker, Wise, and Company, 1863).

14. Thayer, *The Character and Public Services of Abraham Lincoln*, 9.
15. Victor, *The Private and Public Life of Abraham Lincoln*, ix.
16. Williamson, *The Life and Public Services of Abraham Lincoln*, 177.
17. Raymond, *History of the Administration of President Lincoln*, 476–77.
18. Union League of Philadelphia, *Address*, 17.
19. Barrett, *Life of Abraham Lincoln*, 479.
20. *A Workingman's Reasons for the Re-Election of Abraham Lincoln*, 4.
21. Raymond, *The Life of Abraham Lincoln*, 79.
22. Thayer, *The Character and Public Services of Abraham Lincoln*, 31.
23. Raymond, *History of the Administration of Abraham Lincoln*, 479; Thayer, *The Character and Public Services of Abraham Lincoln*, 20.
24. Thayer, *The Character and Public Services of Abraham Lincoln*, 17, 19.
25. For Lincoln's relationship with the Union Army, see James M. McPherson, *Tried by War: Abraham Lincoln as Commander in Chief* (New York: Penguin Press, 2008), 249; and William C. Davis, *Lincoln's Men: How President Lincoln became a Father to an Army and a Nation* (New York: Free Press, 1999).
26. Thayer, *The Character and Public Services of Abraham Lincoln*, 32, 35–36, 39.
27. Barrett, *Life of Abraham Lincoln*, 417.
28. Raymond, *The Life of Abraham Lincoln*, 58–59.
29. Williamson, *The Life and Public Services of Abraham Lincoln*, 131.
30. Raymond, *The Life of Abraham Lincoln*, 81; Thayer, *The Character and Public Services of Abraham Lincoln*, 49.
31. Barrett, *Life of Abraham Lincoln*, 419; Thayer, *The Character and Public Services of Abraham Lincoln*, 49.
32. *A Workingman's Reasons*, 2.
33. Ibid., 6–7.
34. Union League of Philadelphia, *Address*, 3–4.
35. Thayer, *The Character and Public Services of Abraham Lincoln*, 68, 71–72
36. Williamson, *The Life and Public Services of Abraham Lincoln*, 178–80.
37. [Delmar], *Abraham Africanus I. His Secret Life, as Revealed under Mesmeric Influence. Mysteries of the White House* (New York: J. F. Feeks, 1864); *The Lincoln Catechism wherein the Eccentricities & Beauties of Despotism are Fully Set Forth* (New York: J. F. Feeks, 1964.), 1, 21. J. R. Robertson, *The Life of Hon. Alex. Del Mar, formerly Director of the Bureau of Statistics of the United States* (London: E. F. Gooch, 1881).
38. Weber, *Copperheads*, 166–72; Sears, *George B. McClellan*, 368–69, 37.

39. Sears, *George B. McClellan*, 381.
40. Markenfield Addey, *"Little Mac," and How He Became a Great General: A Life of George Brinton McClellan, for Young Americans* (New York: James G. Gregory, 1864); *A Brief Sketch of the Life and History of General McClellan, with Incidents in His Illustrious Career* (New York, 1864); Alexander Delmar, *The Life of George B. McClellan* (New York: T. R. Dawley, 1864); James Gallatin, *Address of Hon. James Gallatin, before the Democratic Union Association, October 18, 1864. George B. McClellan as a Patriot, a Warrior, and a Statesman* (n.p., 1864); G. S. Hillard, *Life and Campaigns of George B. McClellan Major-General U. S. Army* (Philadelphia: J. B. Lippincott & Company, 1864); William Henry Hulbert, *General McClellan and the Conduct of the War* (New York: Sheldon and Company, 1864); and *The Life and Public Services of Gen. Geo. B. McClellan. Campaign Document, No. 4* (New York: Rand & Avery, 1864); *The Life, Campaigns and Public Services of Major General Geo. B. McClellan the Democratic Candidate for President. . . . Written by a Gentleman who accompanied Him through His Campaigns* (Philadelphia: Martin & Randall, 1864); *The Life, Campaigns, and Public Services of General McClellan. The Hero of Western Virginia! South Mountain! and Antietam!* (Philadelphia: T. B. Peterson & Brothers, 1864); Hiatt, *The Political Manual*, 155–58. Anti-McClellan biographies are William Swinton, *McClellan's Military Career Reviewed and Exposed: The Military Policy of the Administration Set Forth and Vindicated* (Washington: Union Congressional Committee, 1864); and George Wilkes, *"McClellan:" Who He Is and "What He Has Done," and Little Mac "From Ball's Bluff to Antietam."* (New York: American News Company, 1864). As is the case with Lincoln's 1864 biographies, I disagree with Miles, who lists several McClellan biographies that I don't consider falling under the definition of "campaign biographies." Miles, *The Image Makers*, 76–79.
41. Hillard, *Life and Campaigns of George B. McClellan*, 358–59.
42. *The Life, Campaigns & Public Services of Major General Geo. B. McClellan*, 76.
43. Ibid., 76–77.
44. Delmar, *The Life of George B. McClellan*, 106.
45. Gallatin, *Address*, 8–9.
46. Ibid., 6–7.
47. *The Life, Campaigns & Public Services of Major General Geo. B. McClellan*, 77.
48. Burlingame, *Abraham Lincoln*, 2: 723–24. Concerning the overwhelming soldier vote for Lincoln, Jonathan White argues that many soldiers supporting the Democratic Party chose not to vote in the 1864 election. See Jonathan W. White, "'For My Part, I Don't Care Who is Elected President,'" in *This Distracted and Anarchical People*, 104–21.

Conclusion:
Biographies and Ballots

1. For discussions of the how various images of Lincoln have evolved since his assassination, see Merrill D. Peterson, *Lincoln in American Memory* (Oxford: Oxford University Press, 1994); Barry Schwartz, *Abraham Lincoln and the Forge of National Memory* (Chicago: University of Chicago Press, 2000); and *Abraham Lincoln in the Post-Heroic Era: History and Memory in Late Twentieth-Century America* (Chicago: University of Chicago Press, 2008). See also, Fred Reed, *Abraham Lincoln: The Image of His Greatness* (Atlanta: Whitman, 2009), which focuses on Lincoln's image portrayed in postcards, currency, prints, photographs, stamps, and works of art.
2. The historiography of the 1860 election is reviewed by Douglas G. Gardner, "'An Inscrutable Election?' The Historiography of the Election of 1860," in *The Election of 1860 Reconsidered*, 245–64. For an effort to quantify and account for high voter turnout in 1860, see Thomas E. Rogers, "Saving the Republic: Turnout, Ideology, and Republicanism in the Election of 1860," in ibid., 165–92.
3. In the Appendix to *Year of Meteors*, Douglas Egerton considers possible 1860 election scenarios and concludes that it is doubtful that either Douglas or a compromise Democratic candidate would have defeated Lincoln.

SELECTED BIBLIOGRAPHY

Primary Sources

Addey, Markinfield. *"Little Mac," and How He Became a Great General: A Life of George Brinton McClellan, for Young Americans*. New York: James G. Gregory, 1864.

Barrett, Joseph Hartwell. *Life of Abraham Lincoln, (of Illinois) . . . also a Sketch of the Life of Hannibal Hamlin (of Maine)*. Cincinnati: Moore, Wilstach, Keys & Co., 1860.

———. *Life of Abraham Lincoln, Presenting His Early History, Political Career, and Speeches in and out of Congress; also a General View of His Policy as President of the United States, with His Messages, Proclamations, Letters, etc., and a Concise History of the War*. Cincinnati: Moore, Wilstach & Baldwin, 1864.

Bartlett, D. W. *The Life and Public Services of Hon. Abraham Lincoln . . . to which is added a Biographical Sketch of Hon. Hannibal Hamlin*. New York: H. Dayton, 1860.

Basler, Roy P., ed. "James Quay Howard's Notes on Lincoln." *Abraham Lincoln Quarterly* 4 (1947): 386–400.

Codding, Ichabod. *A Republican Manual for the Campaign. Facts for the People: The Whole Argument in One Book*. Princeton, Ill.: "Republican" Book and Job Printing Office, 1860.

[Delmar, Alexander]. *Abraham Africanus I. His Secret Life, as Revealed under the Mesmeric Influence. Mysteries of the White House*. New York: J. F. Feeks, 1864.

———. *The Life of Geo. B. McClellan*. New York: T. R. Dawley, 1864.

Drew, Thomas, comp., *The Campaign of 1860. Republican Songs for the People, Original and Selected*. Boston: Thayer & Eldridge, 1860.

Flint, Henry M. *Life of Stephen A. Douglas, United States Senator from Illinois, with His Most Important Speeches and Reports*. New York: Derby & Jackson; Chicago: D. B. Cook & Co., 1860.

Fry, William Henry. *Republican "Campaign" Text-Book, for the Year 1860*. New York: A. B. Burdick, 1860.

Gallatin, James. *Address by Hon. James Gallatin, before the Democratic Union Association, October 18, 1864. George B. McClellan as a Patriot, a Warrior, and a Statesman*. N.p., 1864.

Hiatt, J. M. *The Political Manual, comprising Numerous Important Documents Connected with the Political History of America, Compiled from Official Records, with Biographical Sketches and Comments*. Indianapolis: Asher & Adams, 1864.

Hillard, G. S. *Life and Campaigns of George B. McClellan, Major-General of U.S. Army*. Philadelphia: J. B. Lippincott & Co., 1864.

[Hinton, Richard Josiah]. *The Life and Public Services of Hon. Abraham Lincoln, of Illinois, and Hon. Hannibal Hamlin, of Maine*. Boston: Thayer & Eldridge, 1860.
"Hon. Abram Lincoln, of Illinois. Republican Candidate for President." *Harpers Weekly*, May 26, 1860.
Howard, James Quay. *The Life of Abraham Lincoln: With Extracts from His Speeches*. Cincinnati: Anderson, Gates and Wright, 1860.
Howells, William Dean. *Lives and Speeches of Abraham Lincoln and Hannibal Hamlin*. Columbus, Ohio: Follett, Foster & Co., 1860.
———. *Years of My Youth*. New York: Harper & Brothers, 1916.
Hulbert, William Henry. *General McClellan and the Conduct of the War*. New York: Sheldon & Co., 1864.
———. *The Life and Services of Gen. G. B. McClellan*. Campaign Document No. 4. New York: n.p., 1864.
The Life and Public Services of Major-General McClellan. Which includes a Complete Summary of His Report. Written by a Gentleman Who Accompanied Him through His Campaigns. Philadelphia: Morton & Randall, 1864.
The Life, Campaigns, and Public Services of General McClellan (George B. McClellan). The Hero of Western Virginia! South Mountain! and Antietam! Philadelphia: T. B. Peterson & Brother, 1864.
The Life of Abraham Lincoln. New York: T. R. Dawley, 1864.
The Life, Speeches, and Public Services of Abram Lincoln, together with a Sketch of the Life of Hannibal Hamlin. New York: Rudd & Carleton, 1860.
The Life, Speeches, and Public Services of John Bell. New York: Rudd & Carleton, 1860.
Lincoln, Abraham. *The Collected Works of Abraham Lincoln*. Ed. Roy P. Basler. 9 vols. New Brunswick, N.J.: Rutgers University Press, 1953–55.
The Lincoln Catechism Wherein the Eccentricities and Beauties of Despotism Are Fully Set Forth. A Guide to the Presidential Election of 1864. New York: J. F. Feeks, 1864.
Lincoln's Kalamazoo Address against Extending Slavery. Also His Life by Joseph J. Lewis; both annotated by Thomas I. Starr. Detroit: Fine Book Circle, 1941.
The Lives of the Present Candidates for President and Vice President of the United States. Cincinnati: H. M. Rulison; Philadelphia: D. Rulison; St. Louis: C. Drew & Co.; Geneva, N.Y.: J. Whitley Jr., 1860.
Portraits and Sketches of John C. Breckinridge and Joseph Lane, together with the National Democratic Platform. New York: J. C. Buttre, 1860.
Portraits and Sketches of the Lives of all the Candidates for the Presidency and Vice Presidency, for 1860. New York: J. C. Buttre, 1860.
Raymond, Henry J. *History of the Administration of President Lincoln, including His Speeches, Letters, Addresses, Proclamation, and Messages. With a Preliminary Sketch of His Life*. New York: J. C. Derby & N. C. Miller, 1864.

———. *The Life of Abraham Lincoln . . . and Andrew Johnson, by John Savage.* New York: National Union Executive Committee, 1864.
[Scripps, John Locke]. *Life of Abraham Lincoln.* Chicago: Chicago Press and Tribune, 1860.
Sheahan, James W. *The Life of Stephen A. Douglas.* New York: Harper & Brothers, 1860.
Thayer, William M. *The Character and Public Services of Abraham Lincoln, President of the United States.* Boston: Dinsmoor and Company, 1864.
The Union League of Philadelphia. *Address by the Union League of Philadelphia, to the Citizens of Pennsylvania in Favor of the Re-election of Abraham Lincoln.* Philadelphia: The Union League of Philadelphia, 1864.
Victor, O. J. *The Private and Public Life of Abraham Lincoln comprising a Full Account of His Early Years, and a Succinct Record of His Career as Statesman and President.* New York: Beadle & Co., 1864.
Vose, Reuben. *The Life and Speeches of Abraham Lincoln, and Hannibal Hamlin.* New York: Hilton, Gallaher & Co., 1860.
Warden, Robert B. *A Voter's Version of the Life and Character of Stephen Arnold Douglas.* Columbus, Ohio: Follett, Foster & Co., 1860.
Washburne, E. B. *Abraham Lincoln, His Personal History and Public Record. Speech of Hon. E. B. Washburne, of Illinois.* Washington: Republican Congressional Committee, 1860.
Wells, J. G. *Wells' Illustrated National Campaign Hand-Book for 1860. Part First. Embracing the Lives of all the Candidates for President and Vice President.* New York: J. G. Wells; Cincinnati: Mack R. Barnitz, 1860.
[Williamson, David Brainerd]. *Life and Public Services of Abraham Lincoln. Sixteenth President of the United States, Commander-in-Chief of the Army and Navy of the United States.* Philadelphia: T. B. Peterson & Brothers, 1864.

Secondary Sources

Altschuler, Glen C., and Stuart M. Blumin. *Rude Republic: Americans and Their Politics in the Nineteenth Century.* Princeton, N.J.: Princeton University Press, 2000.
Baker, Jean H. *"Not Much of Me": Abraham Lincoln as a Typical American.* Fort Wayne, Ind.: Louis A. Warren Lincoln Library and Museum, 1988.
Baldasty, Gerald J. "The Press and Politics in the Age of Jackson." *Journalism Monographs* 89 (August 1984).
Barton, William. "The Lincoln of the Biographers." *Transactions of the Illinois State Historical Society* 36 (1929): 58–116.
Borchard, Gregory A. *Abraham Lincoln and Horace Greeley.* Carbondale and Edwardsville: Southern Illinois University Press, 2011.
Brooke, John L. "To Be 'Read by the Whole People': Press, Party, and Public Sphere in the United States, 1789–1840." *Proceedings of the American Antiquarian Society* 110 (2000): 41–118.

Brown, Richard D. *Knowledge Is Power: The Diffusion of Information in Early America, 1700–1865*. New York: Oxford University Press, 1989.

Brown, W. Burlie. *The People's Choice: The Presidential Image in the Campaign Biography*. Baton Rouge: Louisiana State University Press, 1960.

Bunker, Gary L. *From Rail Splitter to Icon: Lincoln's Image in Illustrated Periodicals, 1860–1865*. Kent, Ohio: Kent State University Press, 2001.

Burlingame, Michael. *Abraham Lincoln: A Life*. 2 vols. Baltimore: Johns Hopkins University Press, 2008.

———. *Lincoln and the Civil War*. Carbondale and Edwardsville: Southern Illinois University Press, 2011.

———. "Lincoln Spins the Press." In *Lincoln Reshapes the Presidency*, ed. Charles M. Hubbard, 65–78. Macon, Ga.: Mercer University Press, 2003.

Carwardine, Richard J. "Abraham Lincoln and the Fourth Estate: The White House and the Press during the Civil War." *American Nineteenth-Century History* 7 (March 2006): 1–27.

———. *Lincoln*. London: Pearson Longman, 2003.

Casper, Scott E. *Constructing American Lives: Biography and Culture in Nineteenth-Century America*. Chapel Hill: University of North Carolina Press, 1999.

———. "The Two Lives of Franklin Pierce: Hawthorne, Political Culture, and the Literary Market." *American Literary History* 5 (1993): 203–30.

———, Jeffrey D. Groves, Stephen W. Nissenbaum, and Michael Winship, eds. *The Industrial Book, 1840–1880*. Vol. 3 of *A History of the Book in America*. Chapel Hill: University of North Carolina Press, 2007.

Crew, Danny O., comp., *Presidential Sheet Music: An Illustrated Catalogue*. Jefferson, N.C.: McFarland & Co., 2001.

Davis, William C. *Breckinridge: Statesman, Soldier, Symbol*. 1974. Lexington: University Press of Kentucky, 2010.

Donald, David Herbert. *Lincoln*. New York: Simon and Schuster, 1995.

———, and Harold Holzer, eds. *Lincoln in the Times: The Life of Abraham Lincoln as Originally Reported in the* New York Times. New York: St. Martin's Press, 2005.

Egerton, Douglas R. *Year of Meteors: Stephen Douglas, Abraham Lincoln, and the Election that Brought on the Civil War*. New York: Bloomsbury Press, 2010.

Etulain, Richard W., ed. *Lincoln Looks West: From the Mississippi to the Pacific*. Carbondale and Edwardsville: Southern Illinois University Press, 2010.

Finkleman, Paul, and Martin J. Hershock, eds. *The Political Lincoln: An Encyclopedia*. Washington, D.C.: CQ, 2009.

Fuller, A. James., ed. *The Election of 1860 Reconsidered*. Kent, Ohio: Kent State University Press, 2013.

Goodheart, Adam. *1861: The Civil War Awakening*. New York: Alfred A. Knopf, 2011.
Green, Michael S. *Lincoln and the Election of 1860*. Carbondale and Edwardsville: Southern Illinois University Press, 2011.
Gross, Robert A., and Mary Kelley, eds., *An Extensive Republic: Print, Culture, and Society in the New Nation, 1790–1840*. Vol. 2 of *A History of the Book in America*. Chapel Hill: University of North Carolina Press, 2010.
Gunderson, Robert Gray. *The Log Cabin Campaign*. Lexington: University Press of Kentucky, 1957.
Harper, Robert S. *Lincoln and the Press*. New York: McGraw-Hill, 1951.
Harris, William C. *Lincoln's Rise to the Presidency*. Lawrence: University Press of Kansas, 2007.
Heale, M. J. *The Presidential Quest: Candidates and Images in American Political Culture, 1787–1852*. London and New York: Longman, 1982.
Holt, Michael F. *The Rise and Fall of the American Whig Party: Jacksonian Politics and the Onset of the Civil War*. New York: Oxford University Press, 1999.
Holzer, Harold. "Abraham Lincoln: The Image." *Lincoln Lore* 1897 (Summer 2011): 1, 3–6.
———. "The Campaign of 1860: Cooper Union, Mathew Brady, and the Campaign of Words and Images." In *Lincoln Revisited: New Insights from the Lincoln Forum*, ed. John Y. Simon, Harold Holzer, and Dawn Vogel. New York: Fordham University Press, 2007, 57–80.
———. *Lincoln at Cooper Union: The Speech That Made Abraham Lincoln President*. New York: Simon and Schuster, 2004.
———, Gabor S. Boritt, and Mark E. Neely Jr. *Changing the Lincoln Image*. Fort Wayne, Ind.: Louis A. Warren Lincoln Library and Museum, 1985.
———. *The Lincoln Image: Abraham Lincoln and the Popular Print*. New York: Charles Scribner's' Sons, 1984).
Howe, Daniel Walker. *The Political Culture of the American Whigs*. Chicago: University of Chicago Press, 1979.
———. *What Hath God Wrought: The Transformation of America, 1815–1848*. New York: Oxford University Press, 2007.
Johannsen, Robert W. *Stephen A. Douglas*. 1973. Urbana and Chicago: University of Illinois Press, 1997.
John, Richard. *Spreading the News: The American Postal System from Franklin to Morse*. Cambridge, Mass.: Harvard University Press, 1995.
Laracey, Mel. "The Presidential Newspaper: The Forgotten Way of Going Public." In *Speaking to the People: The Rhetorical Presidency in Historical Perspective*, ed. Richard J. Ellis. Amherst: University of Massachusetts Press, 1998, 66–86.
Le Beau, Bryan F. *Currier and Ives: American Imagined*. Washington, D.C.: Smithsonian Institute Press, 2001.

Leonard, Thomas C. *The Power of the Press: The Birth of American Political Reporting.* New York: Oxford University Press, 1986.
Lepore, Jill. "Bound for Glory." *New Yorker,* October 20, 2002, 80–85.
Long, David E. *The Jewel of Liberty: Abraham Lincoln's Re-election and the End of Slavery.* Mechanicsburg, Pa.: Stackpole Books, 1994.
McMurtry, R. Gerald. "Campaign Biographies 'Unauthorized.'" *Lincoln Lore* 1434 (August 1957).
———. "Codding's 'Republican Manual for the Campaign—1860.'" *Lincoln Lore* 1490 (April 1962): 1–3.
———. "The Vose Biography of Lincoln." *Lincoln Lore* 1429 (March 1957). 1–3.
Miles, William, comp. *The Image Makers: A Bibliography of American Presidential Campaign Biographies.* Metuchen, N.J.: Scarecrow, 1979.
———, comp. *The People's Voice: An Annotated Bibliography of American Presidential Campaign Newspapers, 1828–1984.* Wesport, Conn.: Greenwood, 1987.
Mitgang, Herbert, ed. *Abraham Lincoln: A Press Portrait.* Athens: University of Georgia Press, 1956.
Morehouse, Francis Milton I. "The Life of Jesse W. Fell." *University of Illinois Studies in the Social Sciences* 5 (June 1916).
Neely, Mark E., Jr. *The Boundaries of American Political Culture in the Civil War Era.* Chapel Hill: University of North Carolina Press, 2005.
Paludan, Philip Shaw. *"The Better Angels of Our Nature": Lincoln, Propaganda and Public Opinion in the North during the American Civil War.* Fort Wayne, Ind.: Lincoln Museum, 1992.
Pasley, Jeffrey L. *"The Tyranny of Printers": Newspaper Politics in the Early American Republic.* Charlottesville: University Press of Virginia, 2001.
Peterson, Merrill D. *Lincoln in American Memory.* New York: Oxford University Press, 1994.
Price, Robert. "Young Howells Drafts a 'Life' for Lincoln." *Ohio History* 76 (1998): 232–46, 275–77.
Sage, Harold K. "Jesse W. Fell and the Lincoln Autobiography." *Journal of the Abraham Lincoln Association* 3 (1981): 49–59.
Schwartz, Barry. *Abraham Lincoln and the Forge of National Memory.* Chicago: University of Chicago Press, 2000.
———. *Abraham Lincoln in the Post-Heroic Era: History and Memory in Late Twentieth-Century America.* Chicago: University of Chicago Press, 2008.
Sears, Stephen W. *George B. McClellan: The Young Napoleon.* New York: Ticknor & Fields, 1988.
Silbey, Joel H., ed. *The American Party Battle: Election Campaign Pamphlets, 1828—1876.* 2 vols. Cambridge, Mass.: Harvard University Press, 1999.
———. *The American Political Nation, 1838–1893.* Stanford: Stanford University Press, 1991.

Temple, Wayne C. "Lincoln's Fence Rails." *Journal of the Illinois State Historical Society* (Spring 1954): 20–34.
Warren, Louis A. "Barrett's Lincoln Biographies." *Lincoln Lore* 853 (August 13, 1945): [1].
———. "Earliest Campaign Biography of 1860." *Lincoln Lore* 599 (September 30, 1940): [1].
———. "Earliest Published Biography Exclusively Lincoln." *Lincoln Lore* 668 (January 26, 1942): [1].
———. "First Issue of Scripps' Biography." *Lincoln Lore* 844 (June 11, 1945): [1].
———. "Lincoln Biographies of 1860." *Lincoln Lore* 57 (May 12, 1930): [1].
———. "Raymond's Lincoln Books." *Lincoln Lore* 848 (July 9, 1945): [1].
———. "Vose's Lincoln—a Rarity." *Lincoln Lore* 419 (April 19, 1937): [1].
Waugh, John C. *Reelecting Lincoln: The Battle for the 1864 Presidency.* New York: Crown, 1997.
Wessen, Ernst James. "Campaign Lives of Abraham Lincoln, 1860." *Papers in Illinois History and Transactions for the Year 1937,* 188–220.
Wilentz, Sean. *The Rise of American Democracy: Jefferson to Lincoln.* New York: W. W. Norton, 2005.
Wynne, Patricia Hochwalt. "Lincoln's Western Image in the 1860 Campaign." *Maryland Historical Magazine* 59 (1964): 165–81.

INDEX

Italicized page numbers indicate figures.

Abbott, Abbot A., 83
A. B. Burdick, 56
Abraham Africanus I (Delmar), 94, *95*
Abraham Lincoln, His Personal History and Public Record (Washburne), 50
advertisements, 34, 45–46
"almanac" trial, 65–66
American System, 9, 66
ancestry of candidates, in campaign biographies, 41, 58–60
Argus of Western America (newspaper), 14
Armstrong, Jack, 62–63
Atlanta, Sherman's capture of, 79, 96
authors of Lincoln's 1860 campaign biographies, 46. *See also names of individual authors*
autobiographical sketches by Lincoln, 54, 57–59

Barrett, Joseph Hartwell: campaign biography (1864) by, 83; on Emancipation Proclamation, 90; *Life of Abraham Lincoln*, 53, 54; on Lincoln as a lawyer, 66; on Lincoln-Douglas debates, 67–68; on Lincoln's character, 61, 71, 88–89; on Lincoln's lineage, 58; on Lincoln's military experience, 63; on Lincoln's political career, 66–67; on Lincoln's suspension of writ of habeas corpus, 91; on Mary Lincoln, 69; political appointment, 54
Bartlett, David W.: basis of campaign biography by, 48; *The Life and Public Services of Hon. Abraham Lincoln*, 47–48; on Lincoln and slavery, 67; on Lincoln as a lawyer, 65; on Lincoln's Christianity, 69
Beadle and Company's Dime Biographical Library, 83
Bell, John, 25, 30–31, 72, 75–76

Berry, William F., 65
biographical material, in campaign biographies, 46–47
biography genre, in nineteenth-century America, 40–41
Black Hawk War, 30
book trade, in mid-nineteenth century, 11–12
Boston Daily Advertiser, 31
Boston Semi-Weekly Courier, 30
Brady, Mathew, 22, 46
Breckinridge, John C., 25, 72–76
Brown, W. Burlie, 38–39, 44
Buchanan, James, 27, 71
Burdick, A. B., 56
Buttre, J. C., 57

campaign biographies, in general: ancestry of candidates in, 41; biographical material in, 46–47; cloth editions vs. paper, 102; for 1860 campaign, 71–72; emergence of genre, 4; format and quantity, 45–46; formative years of candidates in, 42; of incumbents, 103; livelihood of candidates in, 43; military experience of candidates in, 42–43, 63–64; political careers of candidates in, 43; production and dissemination of, 16–17, 37–40; purpose of, 36–37; sales of, 104; structure and content, 40; voters and, 102, 105–6
campaign biographies of Lincoln (1860): ancestry, 58–60; "authorized," 52; biographical material, 46–47; courage and physical strength, 62–63; domestic life, 68–69; fitness to lead the country, 70–71; flatboat trips, 60–61, 64; format and quantity, 45–46; frontier upbringing, 60; honesty, 64–65, 71; legal career, 65–66; Lincoln's reluctance to

campaign biographies of Lincoln (1860) (*continued*)
  cooperate with authors of, 54–55; military experience, 63–64; public records, 57; rail-splitting exploits, 60–61; religion, 69; self-education, 61–62; slavery issue, 67; social qualities, 62; sources used for, 46. *See also titles of specific campaign biographies*
campaign biographies of Lincoln (1864): overview, 81; image promoted in, 85–88; purpose of, 77–78. *See also titles of specific campaign biographies*
"Campaign Document" (Thayer), 85
campaigning, public vs. private, 7, 25, 54–55, 73
campaign newspapers, 16
Canisius, Theodore, 20
carte de visites, 19
cartoons, 18–19, 34–35
character, in Lincoln's 1864 campaign biographies, 85–89
Character and Public Services of Abraham Lincoln (Thayer), 85, *86*
Chester County Times, 24, 46, 54
Chicago Press and Tribune: article on Lincoln as source for campaign biographies, 46, 50, 51; endorsement of Lincoln, 6–7, 21; publication of Scripps's *Life of Abraham Lincoln*, 55
Clary Grove Boys, 62–63
Clay, Henry, 9
Codding, Ichabod, 50–51
communications, national system of, 9–11
Constitutional Union Party, 30–31, 73
Cooper Union address, publication of, 20–21
Cooper Union photograph and engravings, 48, *49*, 52, 57
courage and physical strength, in Lincoln's campaign biographies, 62–63
Currier and Ives, 17, 34

Delmar, Alexander, 94, 98
Democratic Party: Baltimore convention, 72–73; Charleston convention, 72; Copperheads, 78, 94, 96; during 1820s, 8; on Lincoln's military service, 30; McClellan as presidential nominee, 78–79, 96–97; rift in, 72–73, 79
Democratic-Republican Party, 8
Derby and Jackson, 45, 48, 73
Derby and Miller, 81
"Discoveries and Inventions" (Lincoln), 19
divine intervention, in Lincoln's campaign biographies, 91–92
domestic life, in Lincoln's campaign biographies, 68–69
Douglas, Stephen A., 8, 25, 67, 71–74, 76. *See also* Lincoln-Douglas debates
Drew, Thomas, *35*

Eaton, John Henry, 37
education of candidates, in campaign biographies, 42, 61–62
elections (1860), 68, 76, 105
elections (1864), 99–100
endorsements of Lincoln, 6–7
engravings: based on Cooper Union photograph of Lincoln, 48, *49*, 52, 57; of 1860 candidates, 57; in illustrated newspapers, 18–19; in Lincoln's campaign biographies, 40, 46, 81, 83, 85; of Lincoln steering flatboat, 34; in McClellan's campaign biographies, 97; "OLD ABE, THE RAILSPLITTER," 34; in political histories, 56
Everett, Edward, 30–31

Farragut, David, 96
"Father Abraham" image, 103
Federalist Party, 8
Fell, Jesse W., 23–24, 54
flatboat trips, in Lincoln's campaign biographies, 60–61, 64
Flint, Henry M., 73

Follett, Foster, and Company, 20, 45, 51–52, 56, 73
formative years of candidates, in campaign biographies, 42
franking privileges, 20
Frank Leslie's Illustrated Newspaper, 18–19
Frémont, John C., 39, 78, 85
frontier upbringing, in Lincoln's campaign biographies, 60
Fry, William Henry, 56

Gallatin, James, 98–99
Grammar (Kirkham), 62
Grant, Ulysses S., 78
Greeley, Horace: Lincoln compared to Jackson by, 29–30; Lincoln's response to criticism by, 21; *Log Cabin* newspaper and, 15; in *"Nigger" in the Woodpile* cartoon, 34–35; political clout of, 14; in *Rail Candidate* cartoon, 34; rail-splitter image emphasized by, 29; reasons for supporting Lincoln's candidacy, 31–32; Scripps's campaign biography of Lincoln, 55
Grobe, Charles, 33

Hamlin, Hannibal, 34, 47, 52, 54, 78
Hanks, John, 1–3
Harper, Sheahan, 73
Harper's Weekly, 18–19, 46
Harrah for Lincoln (campaign), 27
Harrison, William Henry, 15, 18, 20, 39–40
Harrison Melodies (songster), 18
Hawthorne, Nathaniel, 39–40
Hayes, John L., 52
H. Dayton, 45, 48
Herndon, William Henry, 25
H. H. Lloyd, 34
Hiatt, J. M., 85
Hillard, George S., 97–98
Hinton, Richard Josiah, 48–50, 52, 59, 66–67
History of the Administration of President Lincoln (Raymond), 81

"Honest Abe, the Rail Splitter" image, 1–4, 29–30, 34, 80, 101–3
Honest Old Abe (campaign), 27
honesty, in Lincoln's campaign biographies, 64–65, 71
Howard, James Quay, 52, 56, 59–65, 68–69
Howells, William Dean: campaign biography of Lincoln, 58, 60, 65–66, 69, 71; commissioning of, by Follett, Foster, and Company, 51–52; political appointment, 54

ideology of literacy, 11
Illinois Staats-Anzeiger (newspaper), 20
Illinois State Journal, 2, 20
Illustrated National Campaign Handbook for 1860 (anonymous), 56, 58
illustrated newspapers, 18–19
image making in campaign biographies, 26–29, 85–88
images of Lincoln in presidential campaign: American pioneering mission and, 71; construction and dissemination of, 26–29; critics and, 80, 93; as friend of common laborer, 61; "Honest Abe, the Rail Splitter," 1–4, 29–30, 34, 60–61, 80, 101–3; rustic Western, 57

Jackson, Andrew, 8, 29–30
J. C. Buttre, 57
Jefferson, Thomas, 8
J. F. Feeks, 94
J. G. Wells, 56, 58
Johnson, Andrew, 78, 81
Johnston, Sarah, 59

Kansas-Nebraska Act (1854), 8–9, 67
Kendall, Amos, 13–14

Lane, Joseph, 74
Last Rail Split by "Honest Old Abe" (cartoon), 34
Lee and Walker, 32–33
legal career, in Lincoln's campaign biographies, 65–66

Lewis, Joseph J., 24, 46, 54, 68
Life and Public Services of Abraham Lincoln (Williamson), 83
Life and Public Services of Hon. Abraham Lincoln, of Illinois, and Hon. Hannibal Hamlin, of Maine (Hinton), 50
Life and Speeches of Abraham Lincoln and Hannibal Hamlin (Vose), 51
Life of Abraham Lincoln (Abbott), 83
Life of Abraham Lincoln (anonymous), 87
Life of Abraham Lincoln (Barrett), 53, 54
Life of Abraham Lincoln (Raymond), 81, 82
Life of Abraham Lincoln (Scripps), 55, 124*n*22
Life of Abraham Lincoln: With Extracts from His Speeches (Howard), 56
Life of Andrew Jackson (Eaton), 37
Life of Franklin Pierce (Hawthorne), 39
Life of Stephen A. Douglas, United States Senator from Illinois (Flint), 73
Life, Speeches, and Public Services of Abram Lincoln (anonymous), 47, 49
Lincoln, Abraham: attacks on, 21–22, 103; autobiographical narratives, 23–25, 54–55; as autodidact, 19; behind-the-scenes campaign strategy, 25; Greeley's comparison of, to Jackson, 29–30; on importance of printing in history, 19; memorandum to cabinet, 79; nomination of, at Baltimore convention, 78; opposition to candidacy of, 30–31; purchase of German-language newspaper, 20; reelection of, 99–100; as representative American, 70; results of 1860 election, 76; support for candidacy of, 21, 31–32; use of public letters, 21
Lincoln, Benjamin, 58
Lincoln, Mary, 69
Lincoln, Nancy Hanks, 59
Lincoln, Sarah Johnston, 59
Lincoln, Thomas, 60
Lincoln Catechism (anonymous), 94–96
Lincoln-Douglas debates, 20, 50, 66–68
Lincoln Quick Step (Grobe), 32–33, *33*
literacy rates, first half of nineteenth century, 11
lithographic prints, 17–19, 33–34, 54
livelihood of candidates, in campaign biographies, 43
Lives and Speeches of Abraham Lincoln and Hannibal Hamlin (Howells), 52
Lives of the Present Candidates for President and Vice President of the United States (anonymous), 57–58
Lloyd, H. H., 34
Log Cabin (newspaper), 15
"Log Cabin" presidential campaign, 15

McClellan, George B., 78–79, 96–99
Mexican War, 66–67
military experience of candidates, in campaign biographies, 42–43, 63–64
Missouri Compromise of 1820, 8
Momus (comic paper), 34
Moore, Wilstach, Keys, and Company, 54, 124*n*18
moral virtues, in Lincoln's campaign biographies, 68
music, in American political campaigns, 17–18

National Intelligencer (newspaper), 14, 21
National Republican Chart/Presidential Campaign, 1860 (broadside), 34
National Union Executive Committee, 81
National Union Party, 78
newspaper editors, political influence and power of, 13–14, 21
newspapers, alignment with political parties, 12–14
New York Daily Tribune, 14, 21, 31–32, 46, 55
New York Illustrated News, 19
New York Times, 14

Nicolay, John G., 25, 47
"Nigger" in the Woodpile (cartoon), 34–35

Oglesby, Richard J., 1–3, 26
"Old Abe of the West" (poem), 27–29

Peace Democrats (Copperheads), 78, 94, 96
Pendleton, George H., 78–79, 96
penny press, 12
Philadelphia Evening Journal, 30–31
photography, 19, 22, 48, 52
Pierce, Franklin, 40, 48
Pioneer Boy (Thayer), 85
Plutarch's Lives, 55
political appointments by Lincoln, 54–56
political campaigns: accepted practices in nineteenth century, 7; music in, 17–18; public vs. private aspects of, 13, 25, 37, 54–55, 73
political career of candidates, in campaign biographies, 43, 66–67, 74
political cartoons, 18–19, 34–35
political pamphleteering, 15–16
political parties, development of, 7–10
politics and print: in 1864 presidential campaign, 80; intertwining of, 10; overlapping worlds of, 4–5
Polk, James K., 8
popular sovereignty concept, 8, 72–73
popular vote, in 1860 election, 68
Portraits and Sketches of the Lives of All the Candidates for the Presidency and Vice-Presidency, for 1860 (anonymous), 57
presidential candidates: lack of public knowledge about, in nineteenth century, 36; public records of, 57; tradition of disavowing interest in public office by, 25, 37, 54–55, 73
printers, colonial, 10
print genres, in mid-nineteenth century, 14
Private and Public Life of Abraham Lincoln (Victor), 83, *84*

private lives of candidates, in campaign biographies, 43–44, 68–69
public letters, Lincoln's use of, 21
public opinion, print's role in shaping, 19–20
publishing houses, commercial, 17–19, 45. *See also names of individual publishing houses*
publishing industry, following Revolutionary War, 10–12

Radical Republicans, 94
Rail Candidate (cartoon), 34
Rail Splitter (campaign newspaper), 16, 26–28, 116n24
rail-splitter image, 1–3, 29–30, 34, 60–61, 80, 101–3
Raymond, Henry Jarvis: assessment regarding Lincoln's reelection chances, 79, 105; campaign biographies of Lincoln, 81; on effect of Emancipation Proclamation, 90–91; on Lincoln's character, 88–89; political clout of, 14
readers of campaign biographies, 104
reading revolution, 11
Reid, John, 37
religion, in campaign biographies, 69
Republican "Campaign" Text-Book for the Year 1860 (Fry), 56
Republican Congressional Committee, 50
Republican Manual for the Campaign (Codding), 50–51
Republican Party: Baltimore convention, 78; criticism of Lincoln within, 94; image of Lincoln and platform of, 101–2; platform in 1860 campaign, 25–26; task of promoting Lincoln's reelection, 80
Republican Songs for the People (Drew), 35
Republican Standard (broadside), 34
Ritchie, Thomas, 13
Rough and Ready Songster, 18
Rudd and Carleton, 47, 75

sales figures for Lincoln's campaign biographies, 104
Sangamo Journal, 20
Savage, John, 81
Scott, Winfield, 39
Scripps, John Locke: *Chicago Press and Tribune* and, 7, 21, 55; and first biographical account after May Republican convention, 46; *Life of Abraham Lincoln*, 55, 124n22; on Lincoln as lawyer, 65; on Lincoln as self-made man, 70; Lincoln's autobiographical sketch and, 21, 54–55; on Lincoln's flatboat trips to New Orleans, 64; on Lincoln's frontier upbringing, 60; on Lincoln's political career, 66–67; on Lincoln's religion, 69; on Lincoln's self-education and social qualities, 61–62
Sedition Act of 1798, 13
self-education, in Lincoln's campaign biographies, 61–62
Seward, William, 20, 48–50
Sheahan, James W., 72–73
sheet music, 17–18, 32–33
Sheridan, Philip, 96
Sherman, William T., 79, 96
slavery issue, 8, 67
slavery issue, in campaign biographies of Lincoln, 67
social qualities, in Lincoln's campaign biographies, 62
songsters, 18
split-rail fence, as symbol in nineteenth century, 3

Taylor, Zachary, 18
T. B. Peterson and Brothers, 83
Thayer, William Makepeace, 85, 89–91, 92–93
Thayer and Eldridge, 48–50

Ticknor and Fields, 39
Ticknor, Reed, and Fields, 40
True American (newspaper), 45–46

Union League of Philadelphia, 92
United States Telegraph, 14
Upham, Charles Wentworth, 39

Vallandigham, Clement, 96
Van Buren, Martin, 8, 15
Victor, Orville James, 83, 85–88
virtues of candidates, in campaign biographies, 44
Vose, Reuben, 51, 58, 70–71
Voter's Version of Life and Character of Stephen Arnold Douglas (Warden), 73

Warden, Robert Bruce, 73
Washburne, Elihu, 50, 60–61
Washington, George, 42
Washington Globe, 14
W. A. Townsend and Company, 45
Weeks, Jordan, and Company, 18
Weems, Mason Locke, 42
Wells, J. G., 56, 58
Whig Party, 8–9, 15
"Wide-Awake Edition" of Lincoln-Douglas debates, 50
Wide-Awakes, 29
"Wigwam Edition," 47
"Wigwam" Grand March (sheet music), 33
Williamson, David Brainerd, 83, 93
"Wood-Chopper of the West" (campaign song), 28
woodcuts, 18, 34, 40, 46–47, 62, 68–69, 83
Workingman's Reasons for the Re-Election of Abraham Lincoln (anonymous), 83–85, 92

Lincoln and the American Founding
Lucas E. Morel

Lincoln and Reconstruction
John C. Rodrigue

Lincoln and the Thirteenth Amendment
Christian G. Samito

Lincoln and Medicine
Glenna R. Schroeder-Lein

Lincoln and the Immigrant
Jason H. Silverman

Lincoln and the U.S. Colored Troops
John David Smith

Lincoln's Assassination
Edward Steers, Jr.

Lincoln and Citizenship
Mark E. Steiner

Lincoln and Race
Richard Striner

Lincoln and Religion
Ferenc Morton Szasz with Margaret Connell Szasz

Lincoln and the Natural Environment
James Tackach

Lincoln and the War's End
John C. Waugh

Lincoln as Hero
Frank J. Williams

Abraham and Mary Lincoln
Kenneth J. Winkle

CONCISE LINCOLN LIBRARY

This series of concise books fills a need for short studies of the life, times, and legacy of President Abraham Lincoln. Each book gives readers the opportunity to quickly achieve basic knowledge of a Lincoln-related topic. These books bring fresh perspectives to well-known topics, investigate previously overlooked subjects, and explore in greater depth topics that have not yet received book-length treatment. For a complete list of current and forthcoming titles, see www.conciselincolnlibrary.com.

Other Books in the Concise Lincoln Library

Abraham Lincoln and Horace Greeley
Gregory A. Borchard

Lincoln and the Civil War
Michael Burlingame

Lincoln's Sense of Humor
Richard Carwardine

Lincoln and the Constitution
Brian R. Dirck

Lincoln in Indiana
Brian R. Dirck

Lincoln the Inventor
Jason Emerson

Lincoln and Native Americans
Michael S. Green

Lincoln and the Election of 1860
Michael S. Green

Lincoln and Congress
William C. Harris

Lincoln and the Union Governors
William C. Harris

Lincoln and the Abolitionists
Stanley Harrold

Lincoln in the Illinois Legislature
Ron J. Keller

Lincoln and the Military
John F. Marszalek

Lincoln and Emancipation
Edna Greene Medford

Thomas A. Horrocks is the former director of the John Hay Library at Brown University. He is the author, editor, and coeditor of eight books, including *The Living Lincoln*, *President James Buchanan and the Crisis of National Leadership*, and *The Annotated Lincoln*.